The Kunstmuseum Basel dedicates this book to Dr. h.c. Maja Oeri, President of the Laurenz Foundation, as a token of thanks for her extraordinarily generous contribution to the realization of the new building.

Kunstmuseum Basel, New Building

With a foreword by Peter Mosimann and
Bernhard Mendes Bürgi, as well as texts
by Bernhard Mendes Bürgi, Emanuel
Christ and Christoph Gantenbein, and
Mechtild Widrich
Photographs by Stefano Graziani

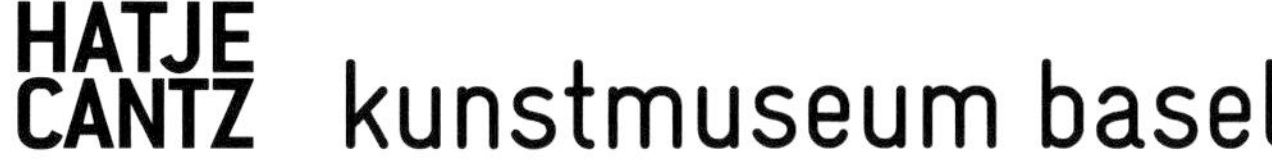

Foreword

Peter Mosimann,
President of the Art Committee

Bernhard Mendes Bürgi,
Director of the Kunstmuseum Basel

This book grew out of the Kunstmuseum Basel's desire to thank its patroness Maja Oeri, President of the Laurenz Foundation, in a manner befitting her unparalleled generosity. Over the years, the Kunstmuseum Basel has benefited a great deal from her expertise in art, her farsightedness, and her uncompromising commitment to the furtherance of the fine arts; and without her engagement, we would not have been able to proceed with such an ambitious, yet crucially important expansion project. Having gifted Canton Basel-Stadt the sum needed to purchase the Burghof site, Maja Oeri also ensured, through the Laurenz Foundation, that the condition imposed by the state was met, namely that half the building costs of CHF 100 million be borne privately.

The dedication of this book to Maja Oeri motivated our decision to make it not so much a compendium of facts and figures, but rather to concentrate on the interaction of art and architecture in the new building. We were, of course, aware that Canton Basel-Stadt would itself be publishing a book on the new building by Christ & Gantenbein, focusing on the making of Basel's most exciting cultural development of recent years, with contributions from a wide range of commentators. For our token of thanks, therefore, we deliberately chose to confine ourselves to only three contributions: from the museum director, the architects, and a historian of art and architecture.

All our activities of recent years have been driven by our determination to advance, promote, and enlarge the Kunstmuseum Basel and its world-famous collection. Our aim has always been to burnish the Kunstmuseum's image as an institution steeped in tradition, which is also dynamic, receptive, and endowed with an identity that is international in thrust, but with strong local roots. It was essential that our collection, our exhibitions, and our outstanding team have an architectural infrastructure befitting of such a major museum, as only then would we be able to keep pace with the best in class worldwide, while at the same time also taking account of local factors. After all, Basel itself is obviously not a world city, even if its Kunstmuseum boasts a collection that is indeed on par with institutions in Paris, London, and New York. Clearly the Kunstmuseum had to be able to expand, and that as closely as possible to the main building that opened in 1936; which is why the Burghof site presented such a unique opportunity. The new building, moreover, was to be more than just a venue for special exhibitions; it was also to house changing presentations of certain aspects of the collection, making for a steady stream of debut appearances.

The creation of a third premises sparked a reconsideration of our institutional structure and the nomenclature hitherto used, as a result of which the Museum für Gegenwartskunst Basel created in 1980 will henceforth bear the name Kunstmuseum Basel | Gegenwart.

Our sincerest thanks go to the people of Basel, who have once again reaffirmed their near-legendary dedication to art in general and to the Kunstmuseum in particular—as they did in a historic referendum in the 1967, when they agreed overwhelmingly to the acquisition of two works by Pablo Picasso. Thus the motion to approve half the construction costs was passed almost without a murmur of dissent when it came before the legislature in 2010; nor was it challenged in the aftermath, which is why on this occasion there was no need for a referendum.

Thanks are also due to a number of individuals who have supported the new building in a wide range of ways. That our vision has become a reality is thanks in no small part to the city's former Chief Cantonal Architect Fritz Schumacher. It was under his aegis that the jury adjudicating the two-stage competition—among whose members was Nicholas Serota, Director of Tate, London—selected the project submitted by the architects Christ & Gantenbein of Basel. A steering committee was then put in place made up of the heads of the three relevant departments of Canton Basel-Stadt: Councilor Eva Herzog as Head of the Finance Department; Councilor Hans-Peter Wessels, as Head of the Buildings and Transport Deparment; and President of the Executive Council Guy Morin, Head of the Department of Presidential Affairs, to all three of whom we extend our sincerest thanks. We are also deeply grateful to the Building Committee under Rolf Borner of the Finance Department, and the Project Management Committee under Carmen Wehmeyer of the Buildings and Transport Department, who likewise worked indefatigably in pursuit of our shared goal. Informative workshops about many different aspects of the building provided us with an immensely beneficial source of architectural knowledge. The whole process was accompanied by a subcommittee of the competition jury; the expertise of Pierre de Meuron, one of the subcommittee members, was invaluable. While we would like to thank all our staff here at the Kunstmuseum Basel, we are especially indebted to our Project Manager Stefan Charles and Project Coordinator Silvia Pfaffhauser, part of whose remit was to maintain a constant dialogue between the museum and the architects. Special thanks are also due to Emanuel Christ, Christoph Gantenbein, and Julia Tobler for their round-the-clock availability and for their deep respect for art. Knowing that we could rely on their sensitivity to see where the architecture should take second place and where it could unfold its full impact as an artistic form of expression in its own right was very reassuring. Our general planner Peter Stocker and all the contractors involved are also included in these thanks.

This publication would not have been possible without the Stiftung für das Kunstmuseum Basel chaired by Markus Altwegg. In closing, we would also like to thank our authors Emanuel Christ, Christoph Gantenbein, and Mechtild Widrich, our editors Salome Schnetz and Maren Stotz, our photographer Stefano Graziani, and our designer Marie Lusa, the sum of whose efforts is this splendid book published, true to a long-standing tradition, by Hatje Cantz Verlag.

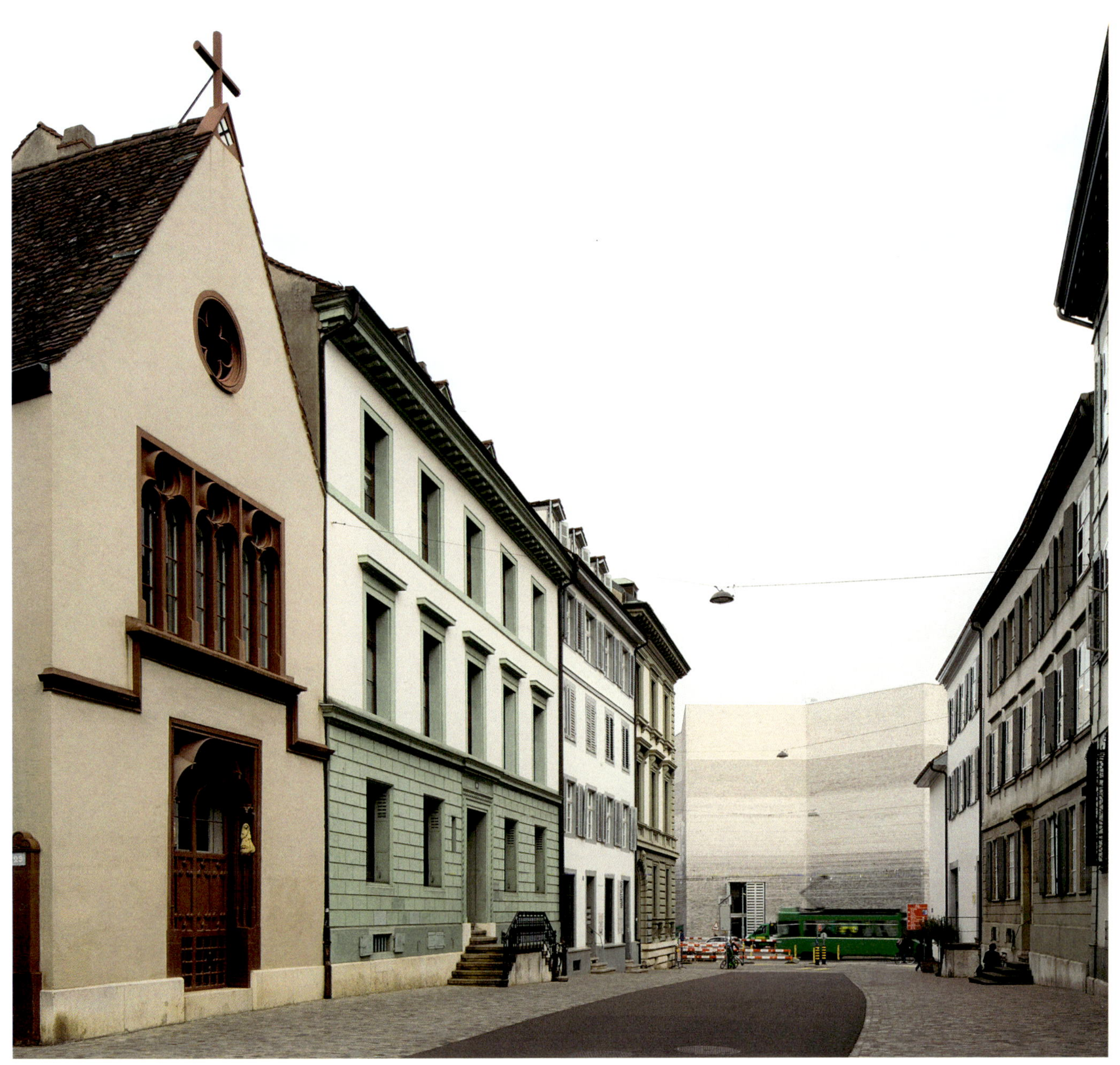

View from Rittergasse

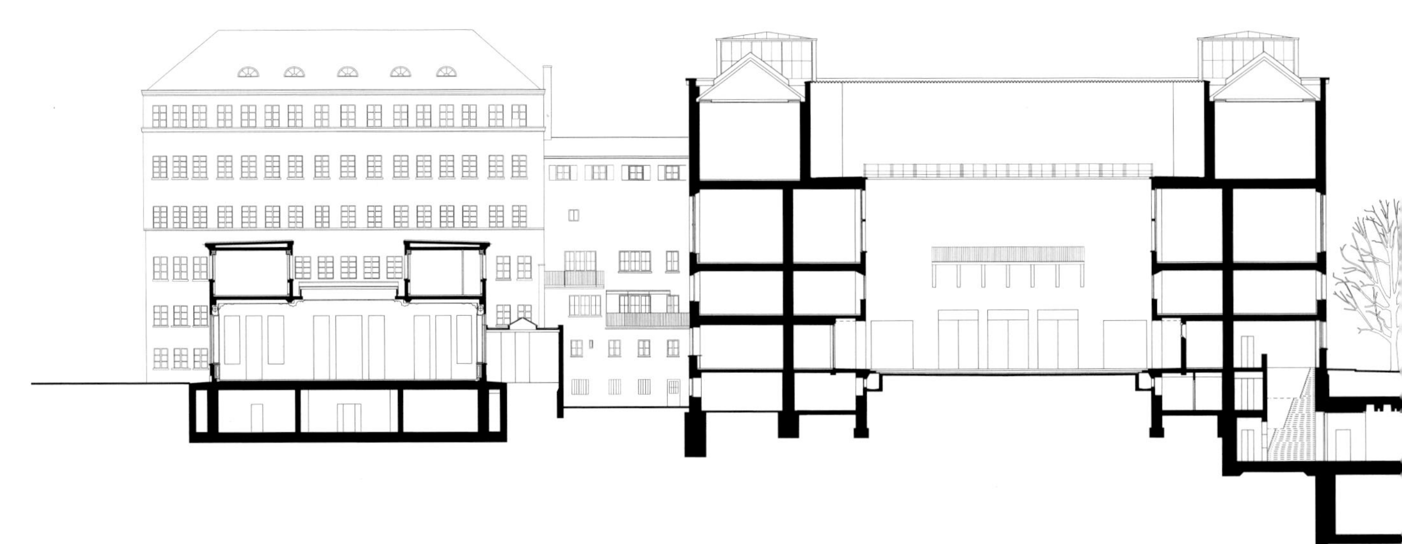

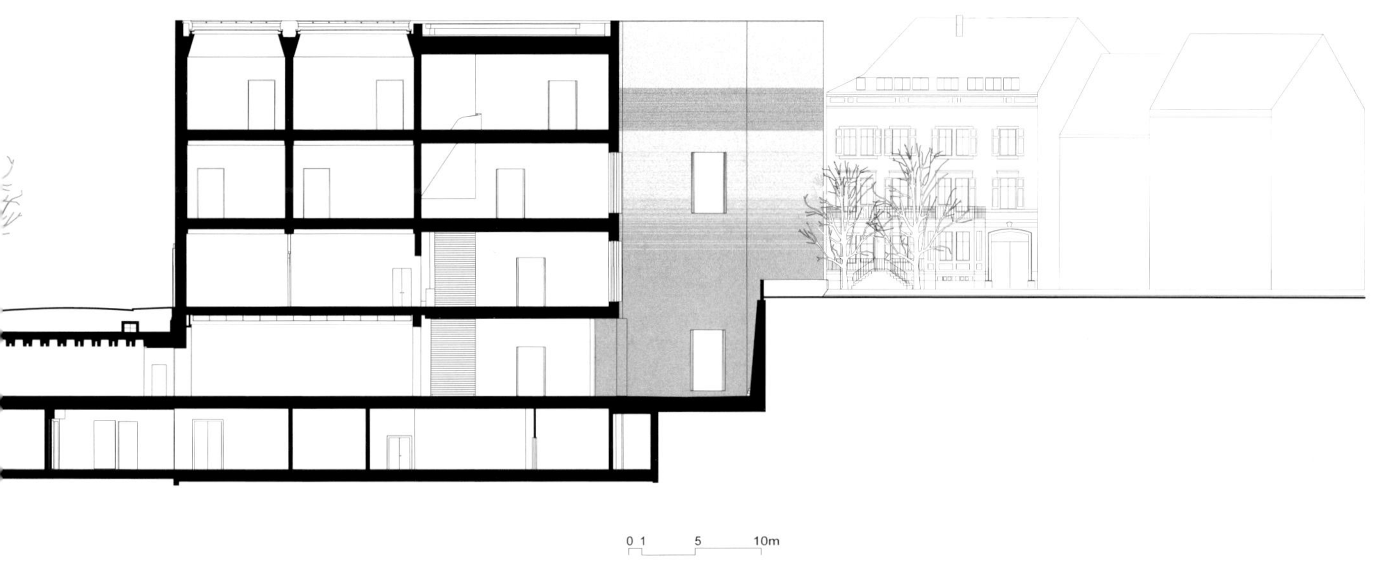

Section through the Laurenzbau with library, main building, and new building

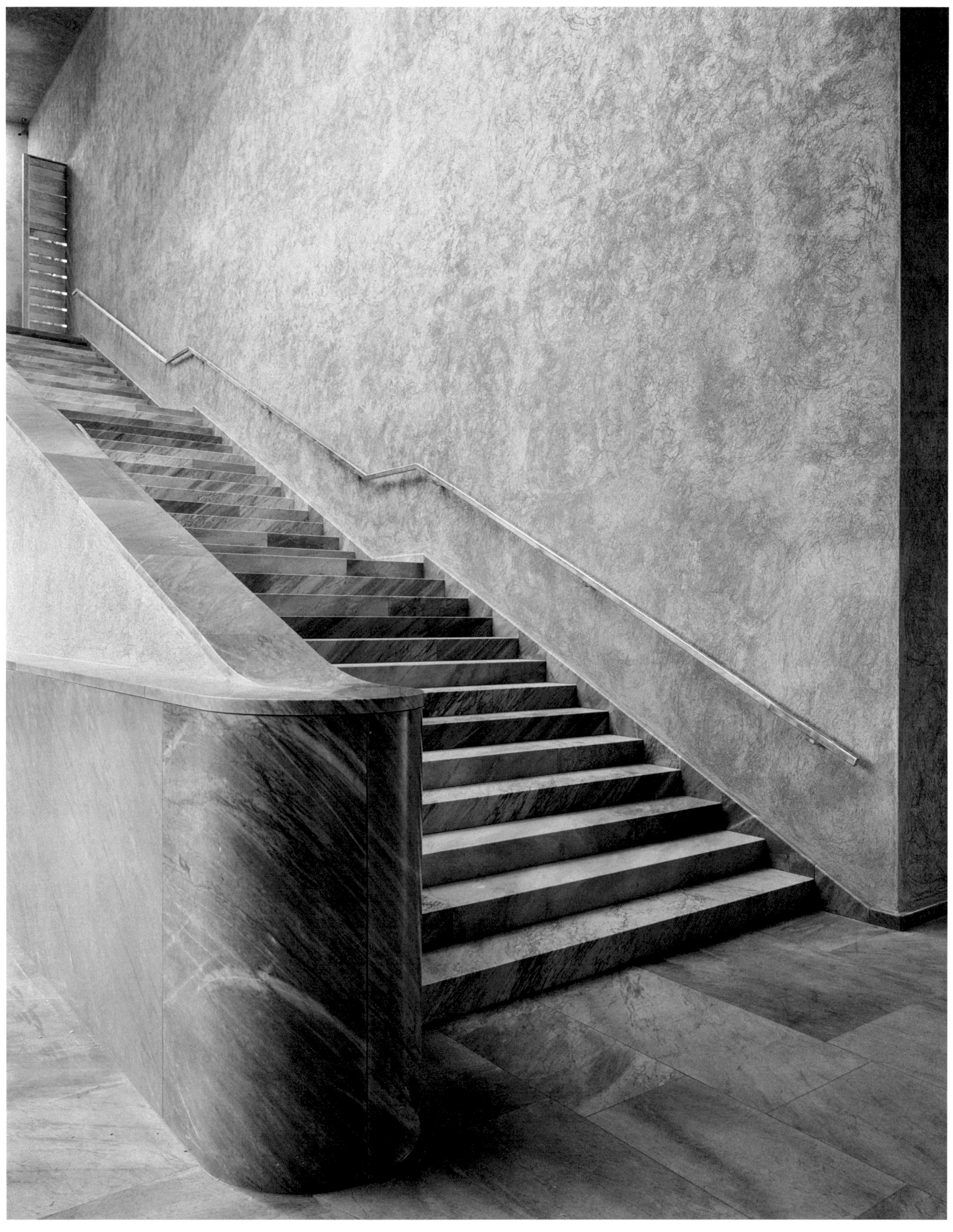

Ground-floor entrance area with marble floor, stairs, and balustrade (Bardiglio Nuvolato from Carrara), scraped plaster walls, and galvanized steel handrail and door

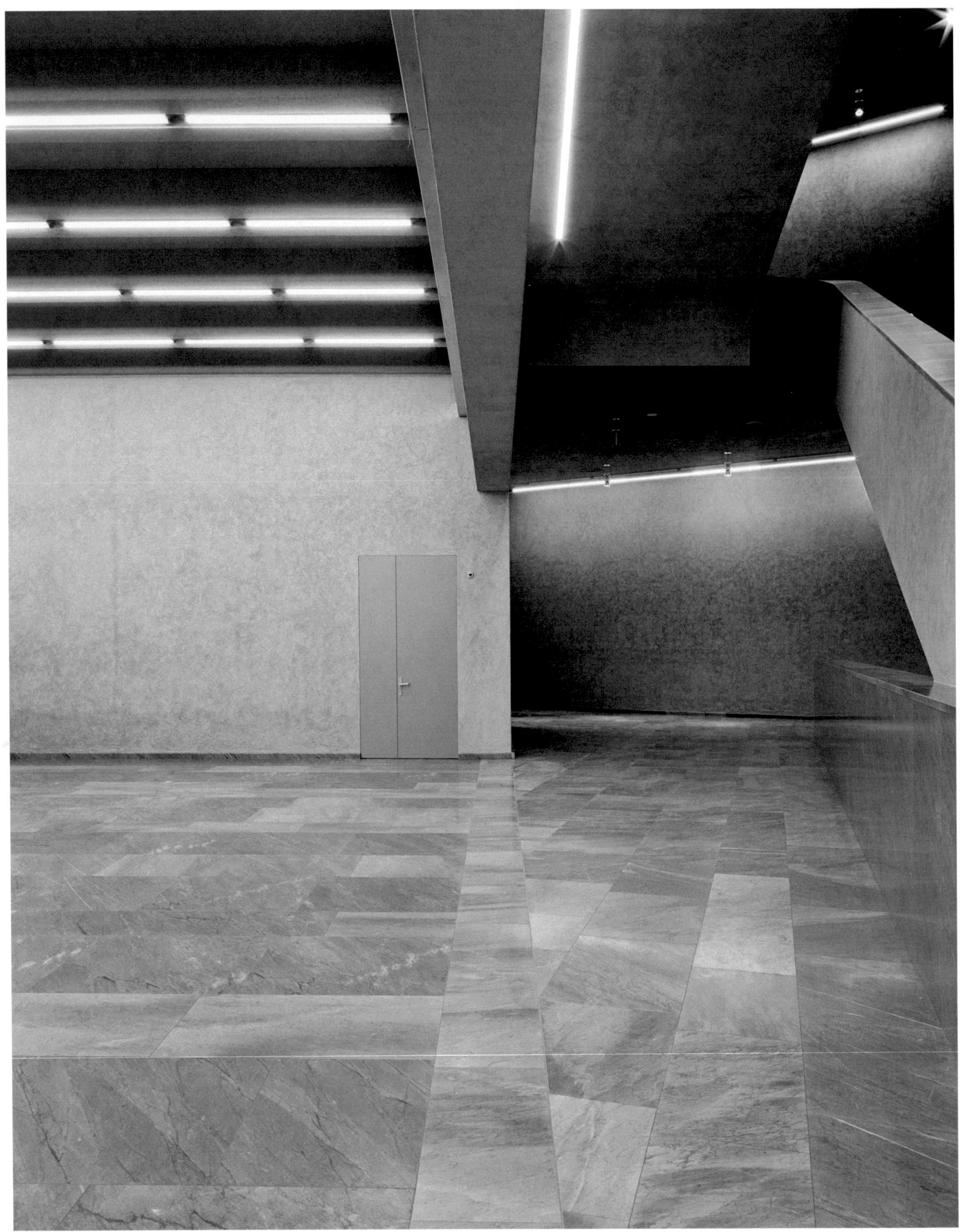

Entrance area

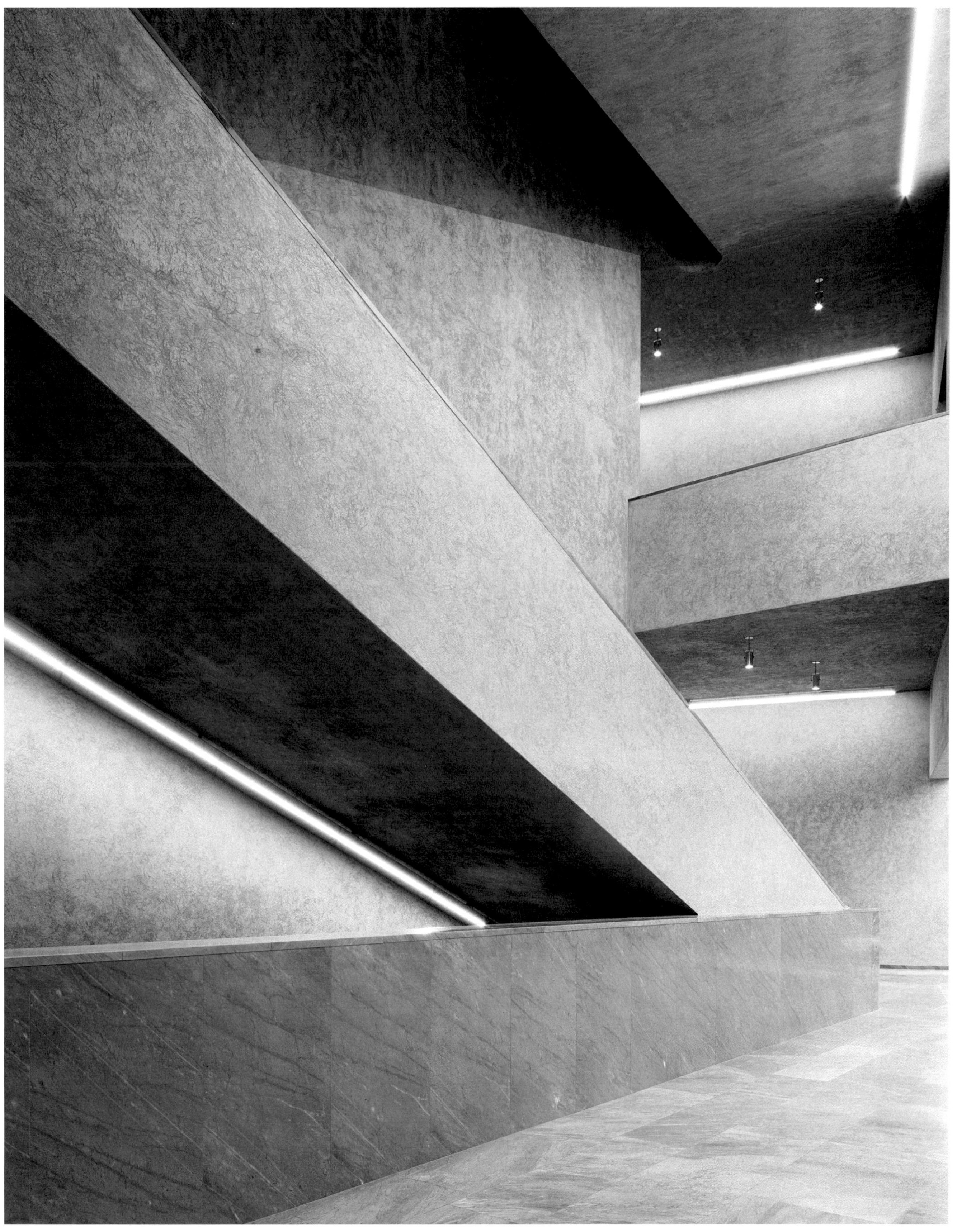

View of central staircase

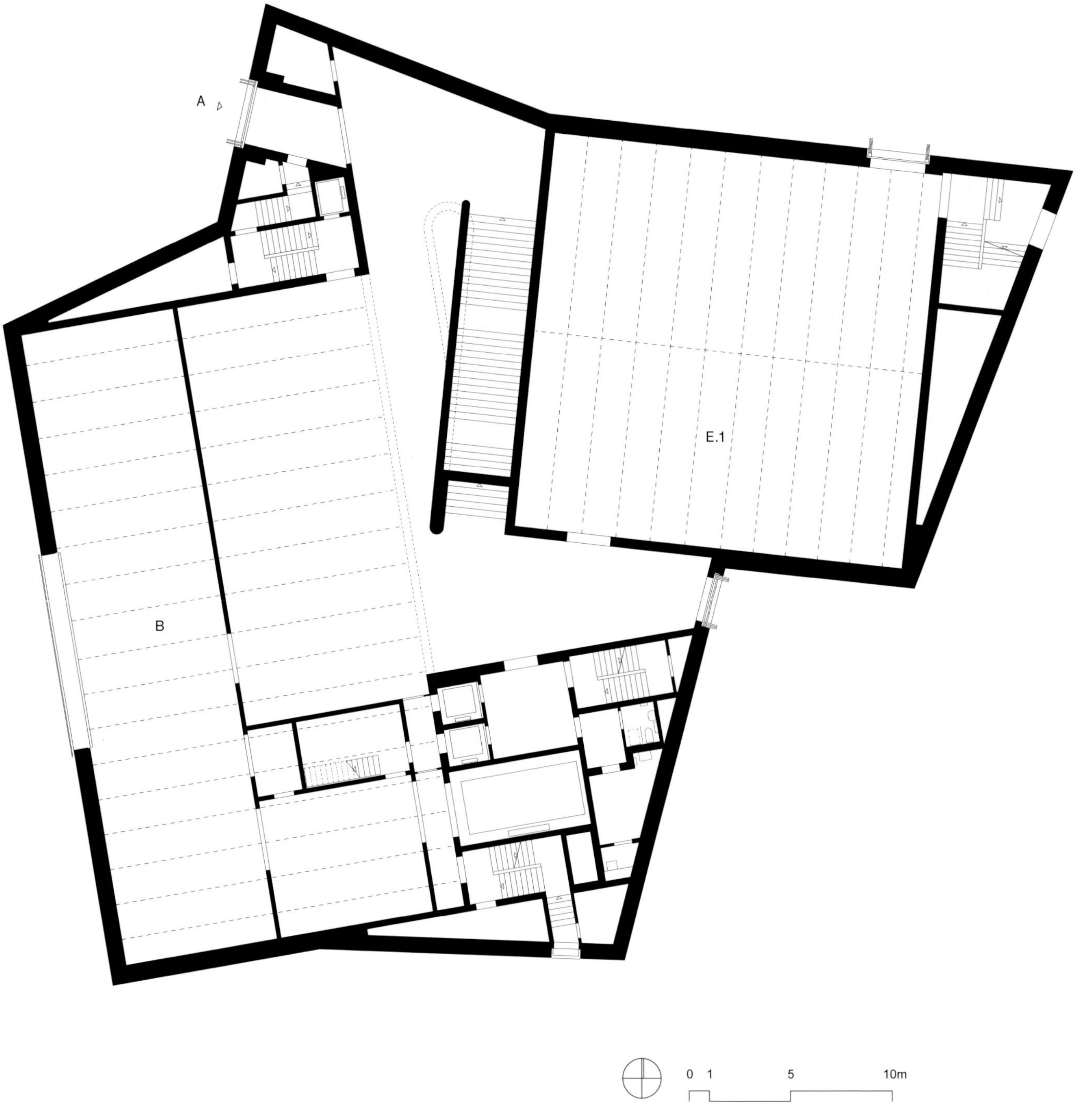

A

E.1

B

GROUND FLOOR
A Entrance / B Deliveries / E.1 Exhibition space

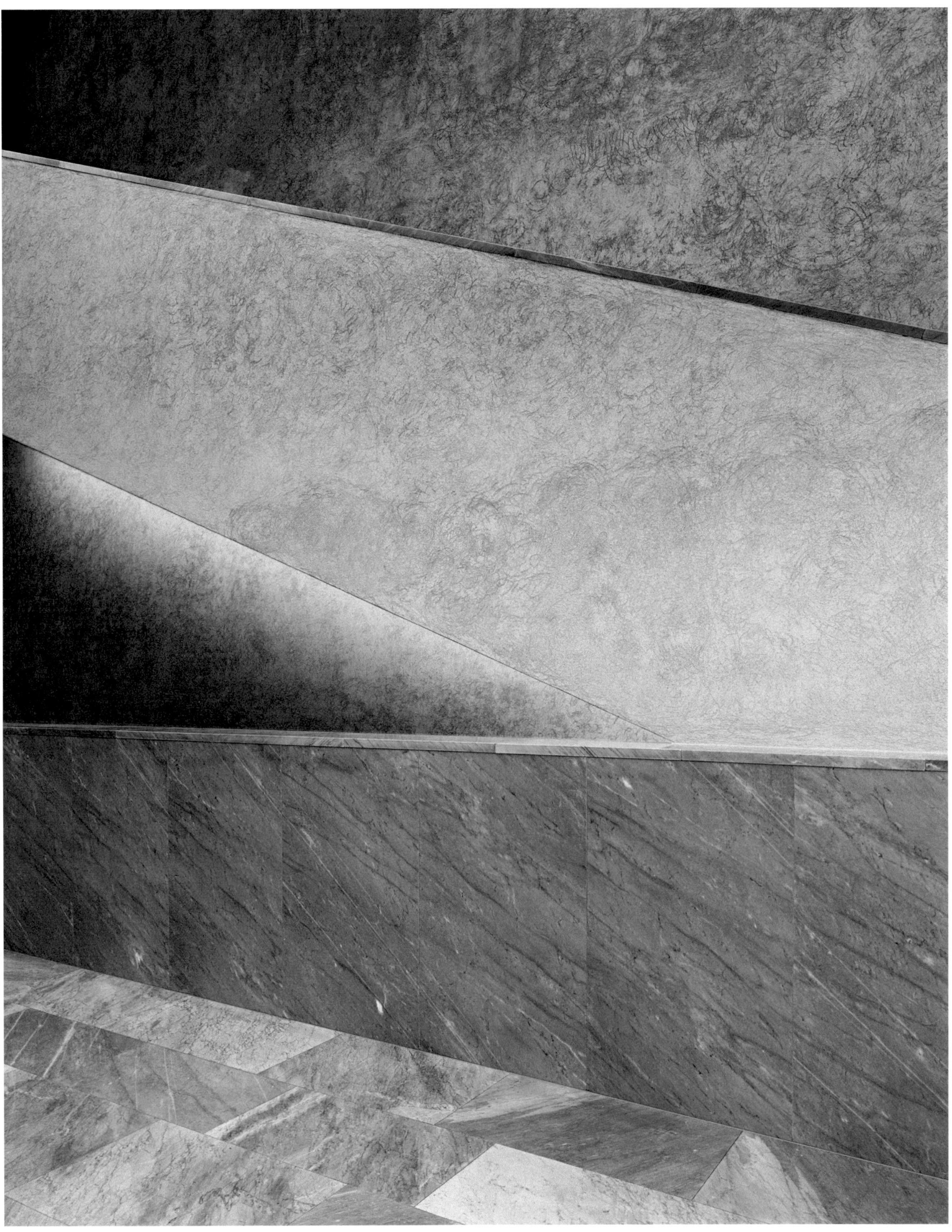

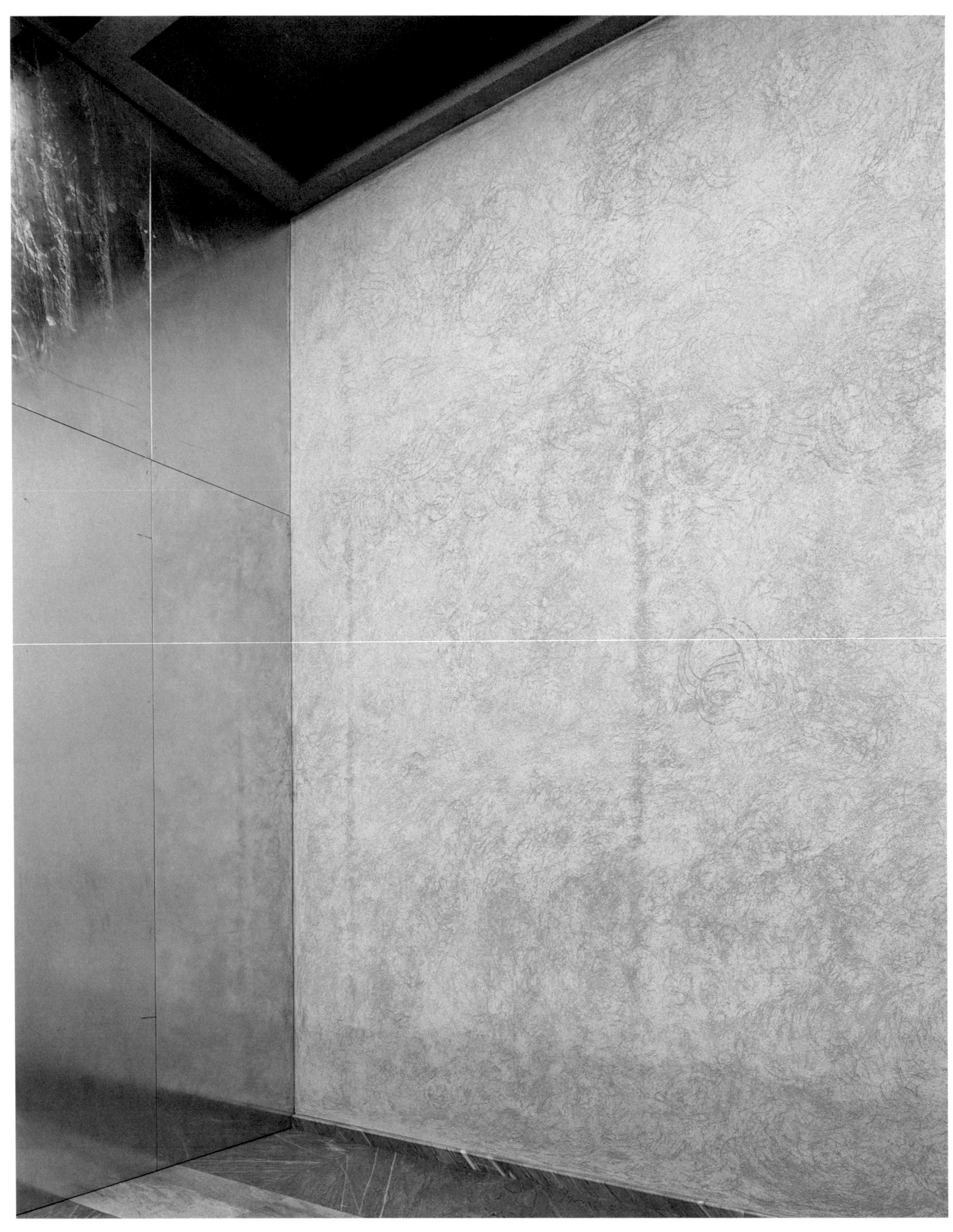

Entrance area with marble floor, scraped plaster walls, galvanized steel clad walls, ceilings with concrete elements and linear LED lighting

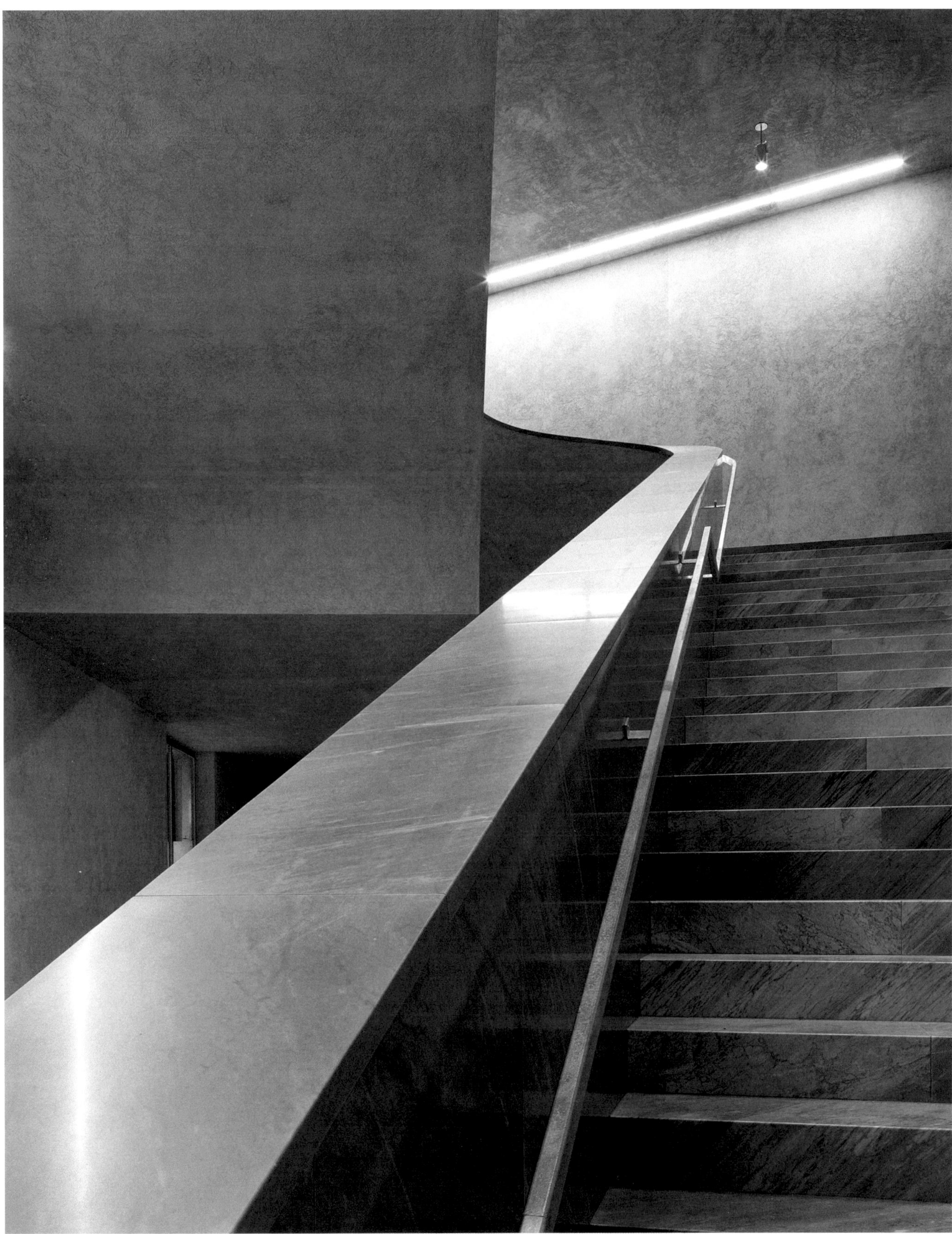

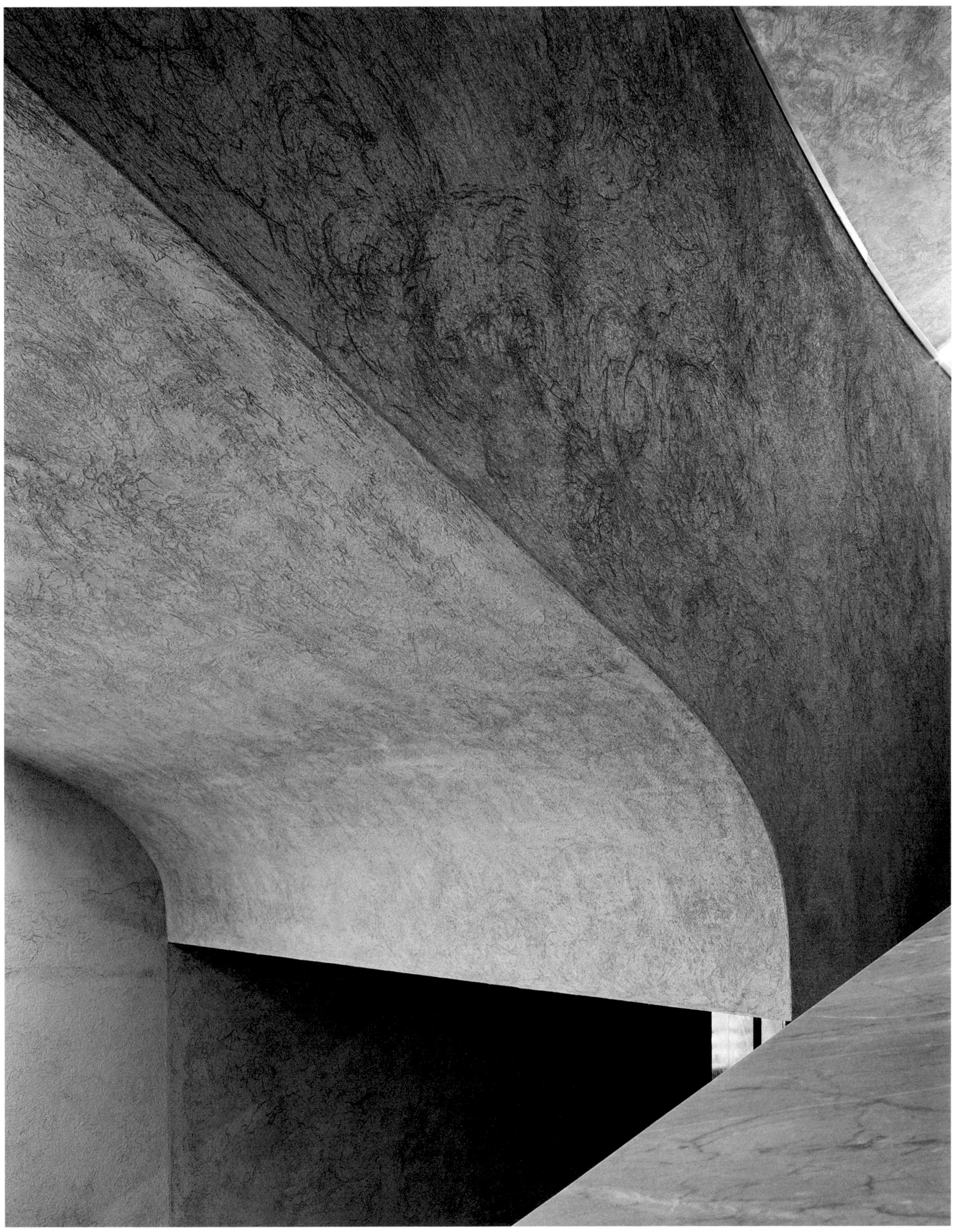

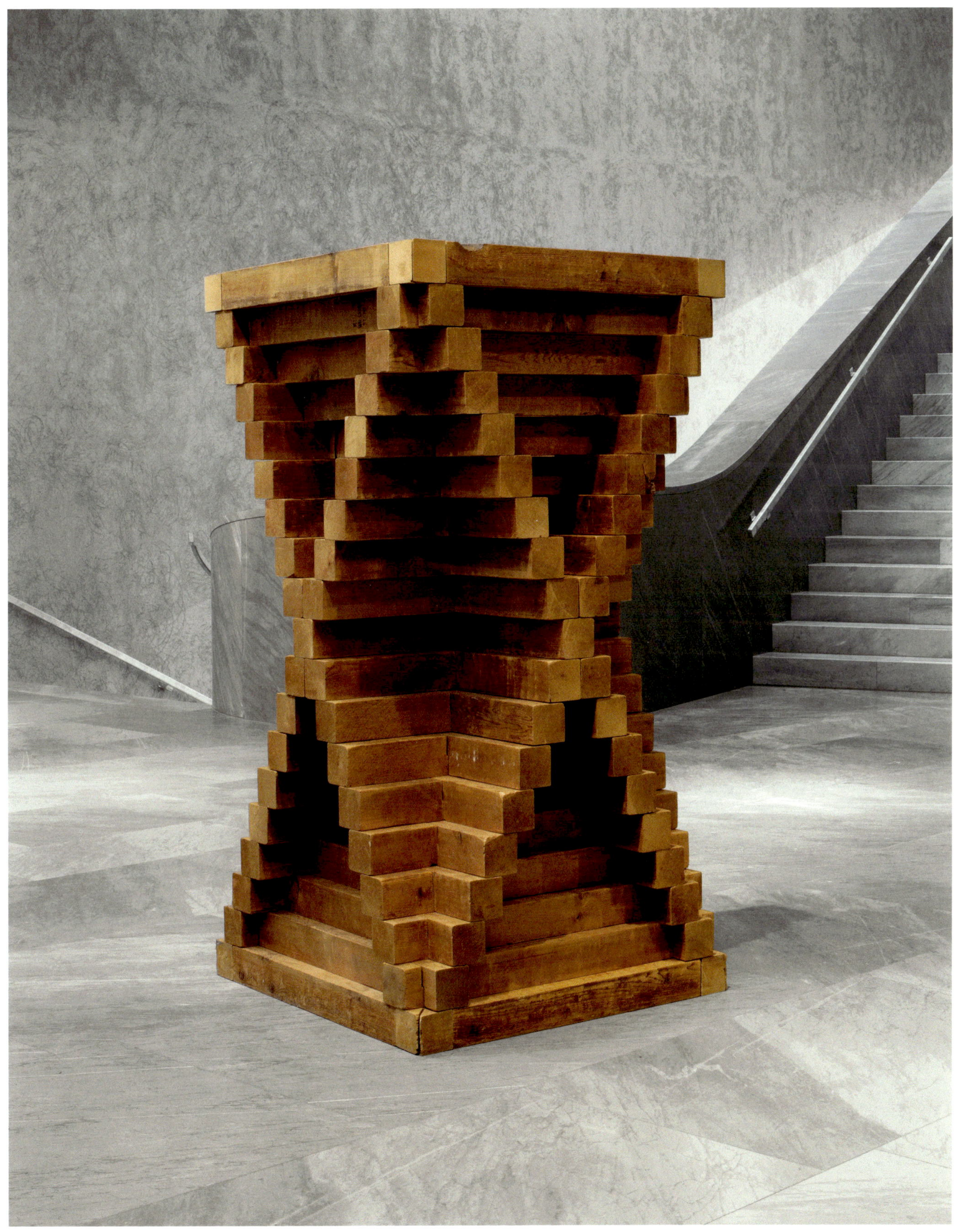

First-floor landing with Carl Andre, *Cedar Piece*, 1959/1964

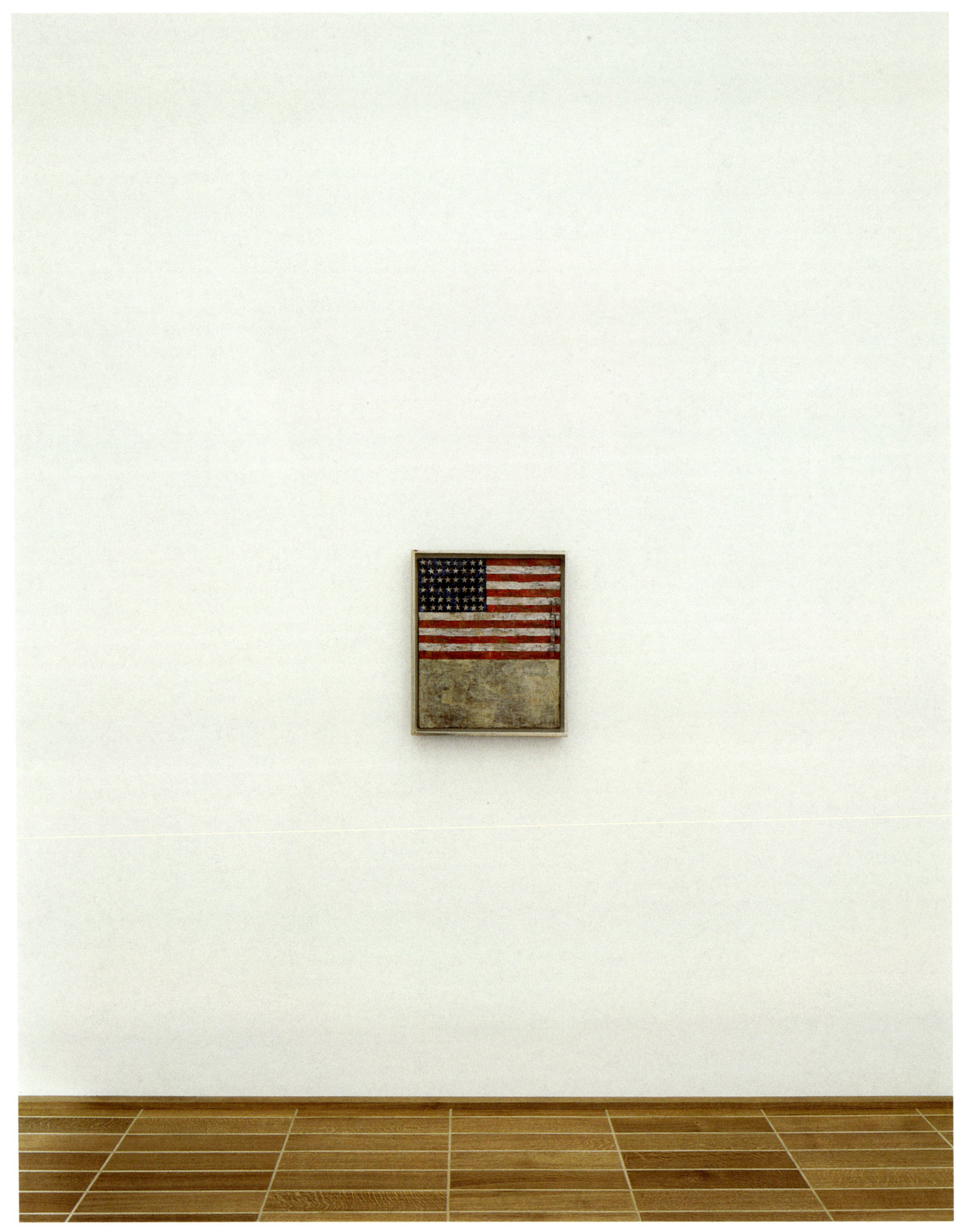

Jasper Johns, *Flag above White with Collage*, 1955

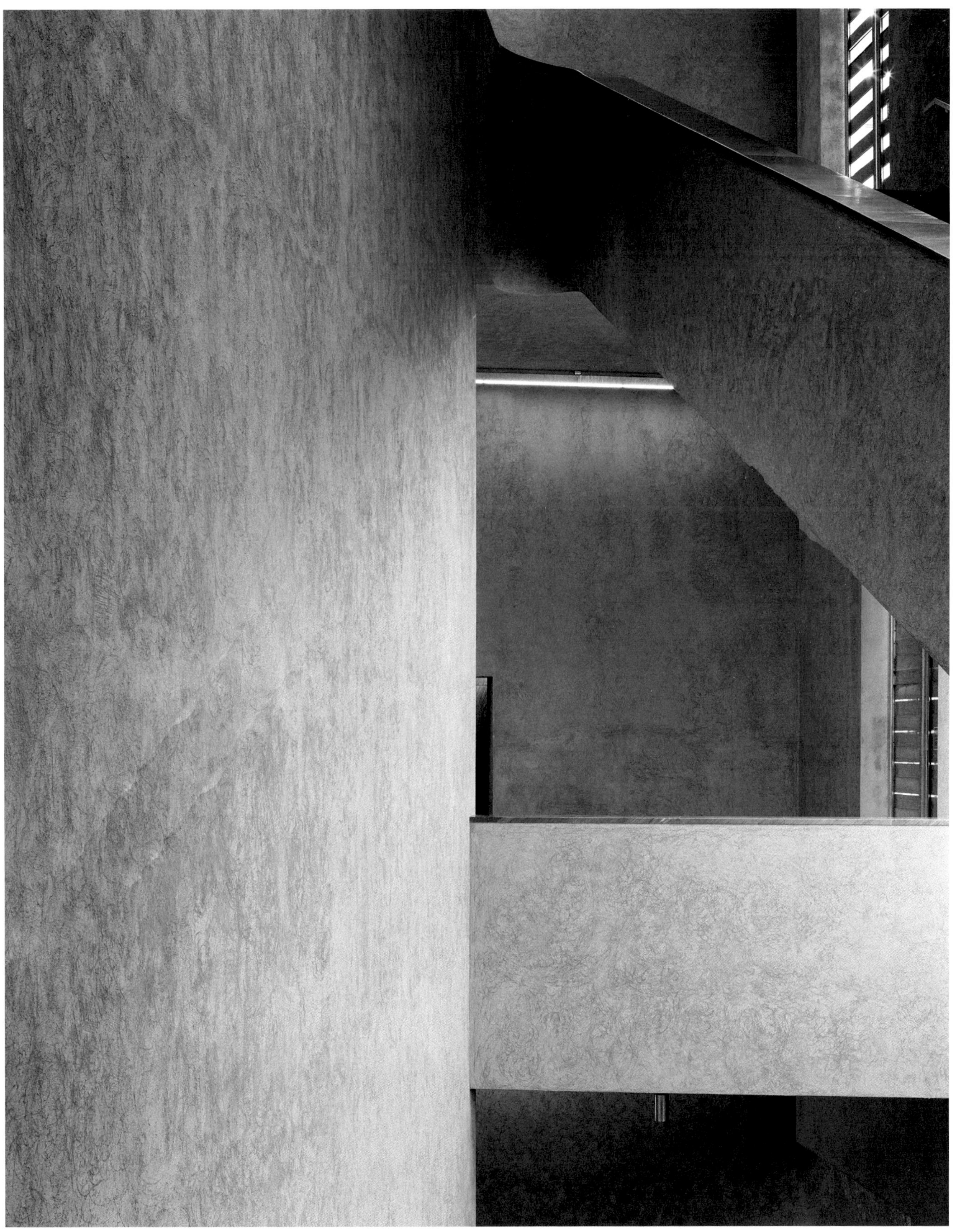

View to the first floor from the staircase

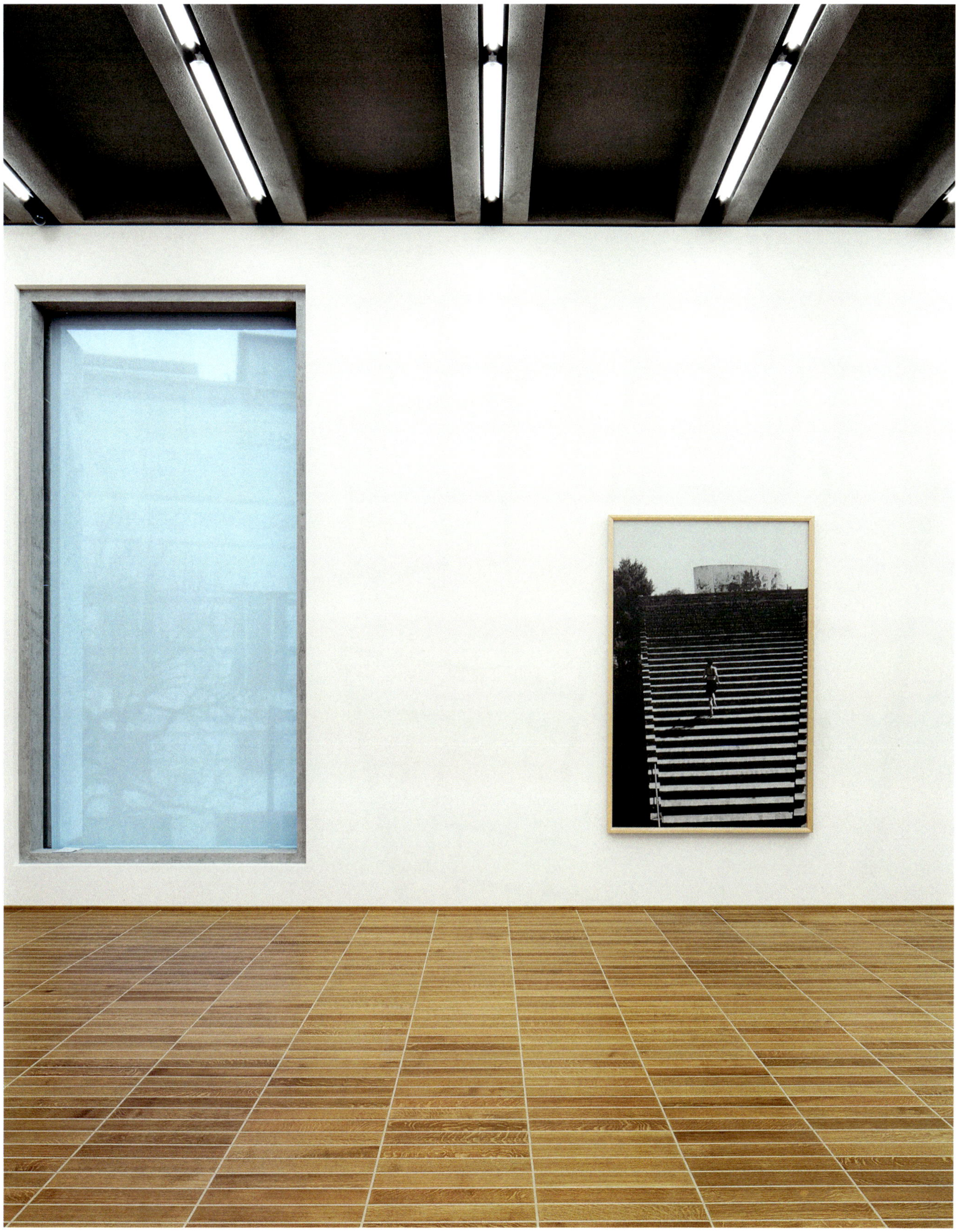

Günther Förg, *Villa Malaparte, Capri*, 1983/2005

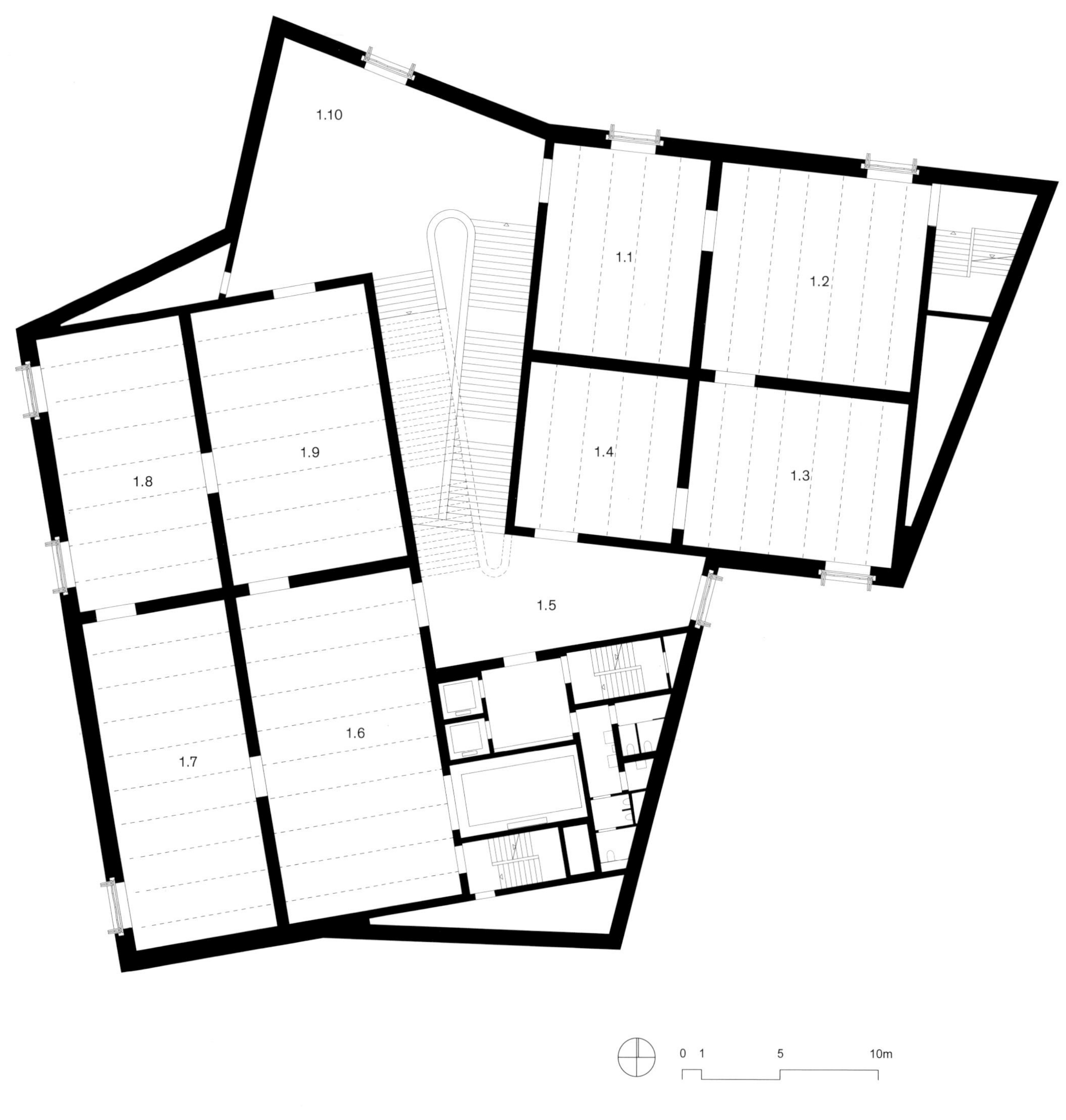

FIRST FLOOR

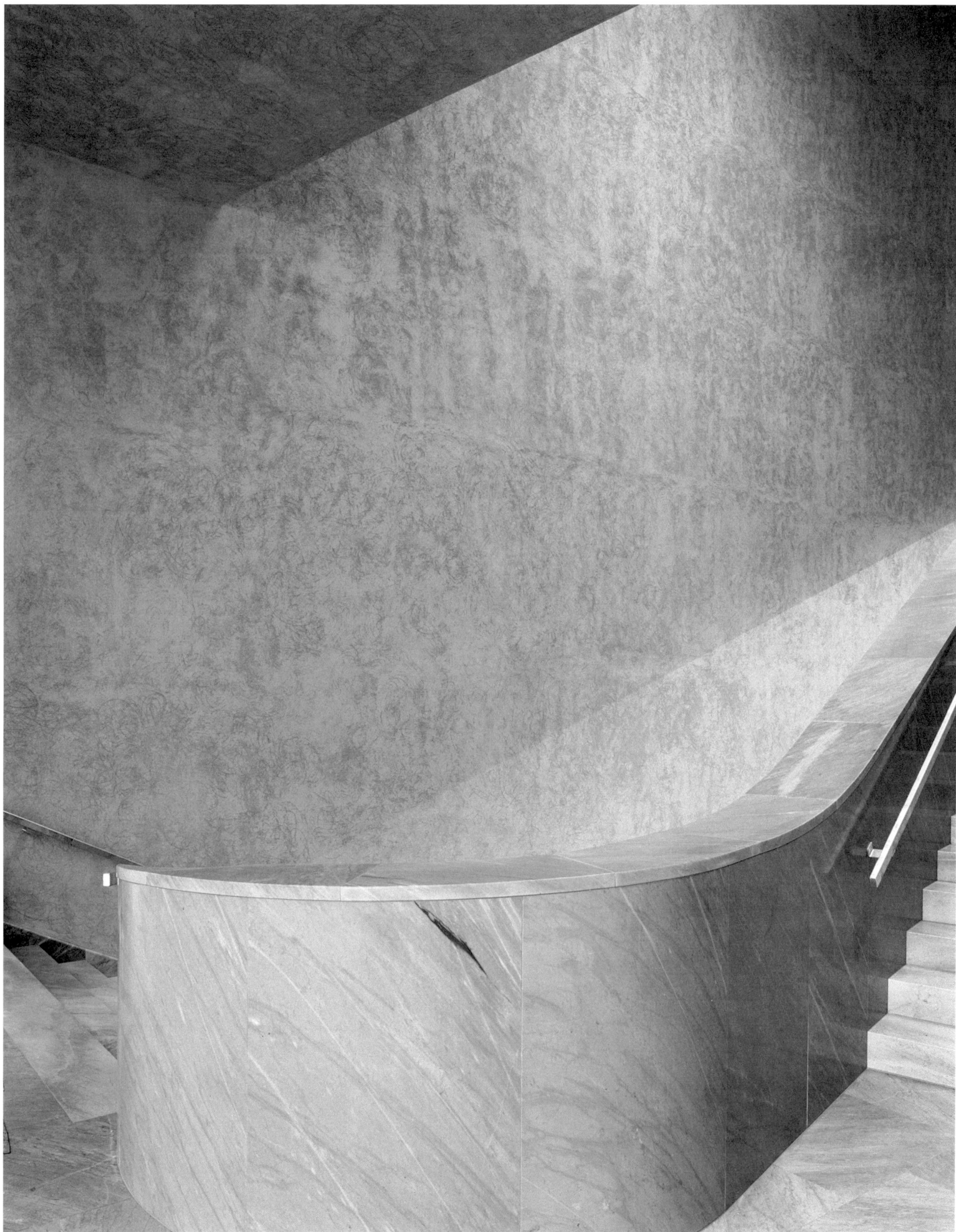

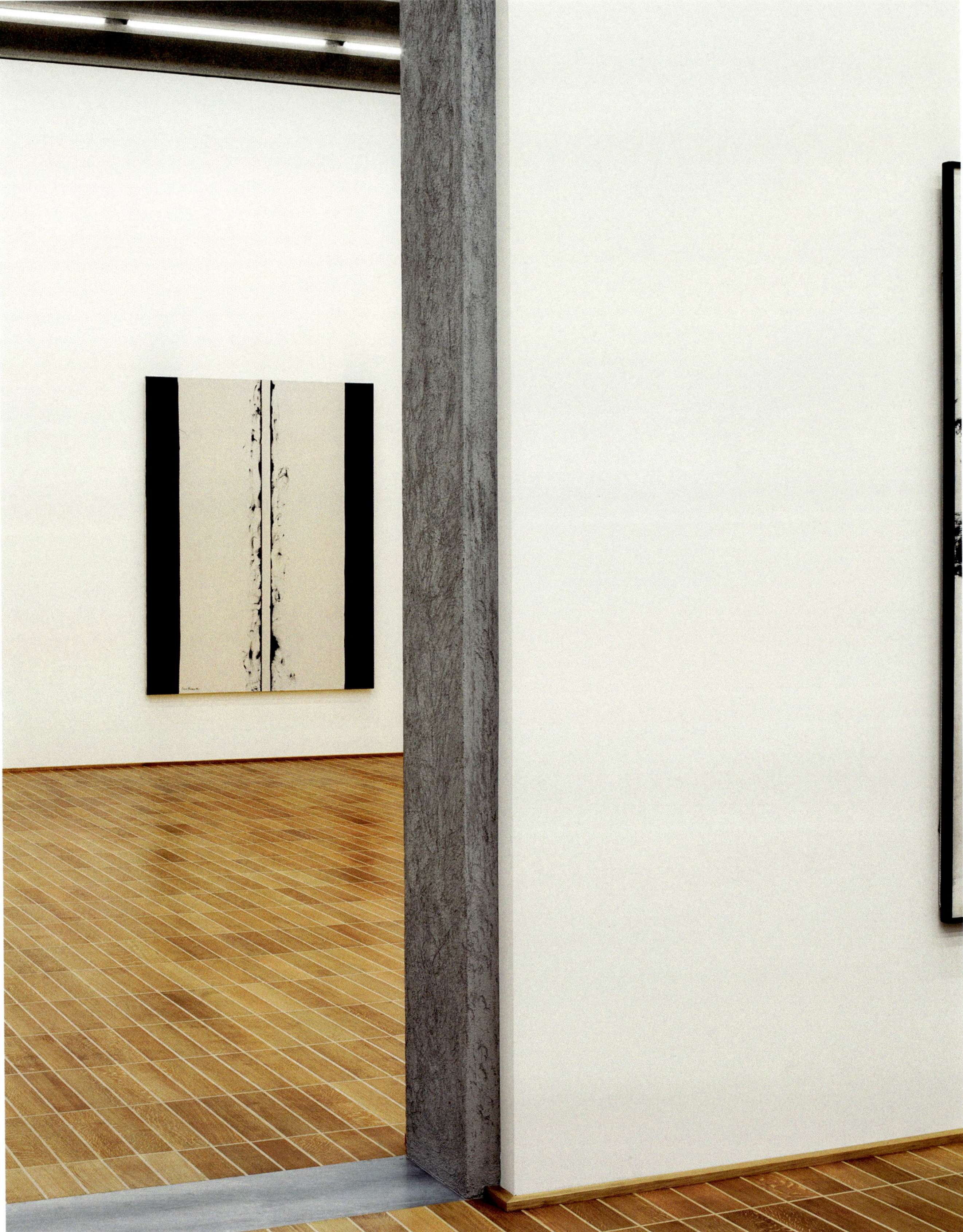

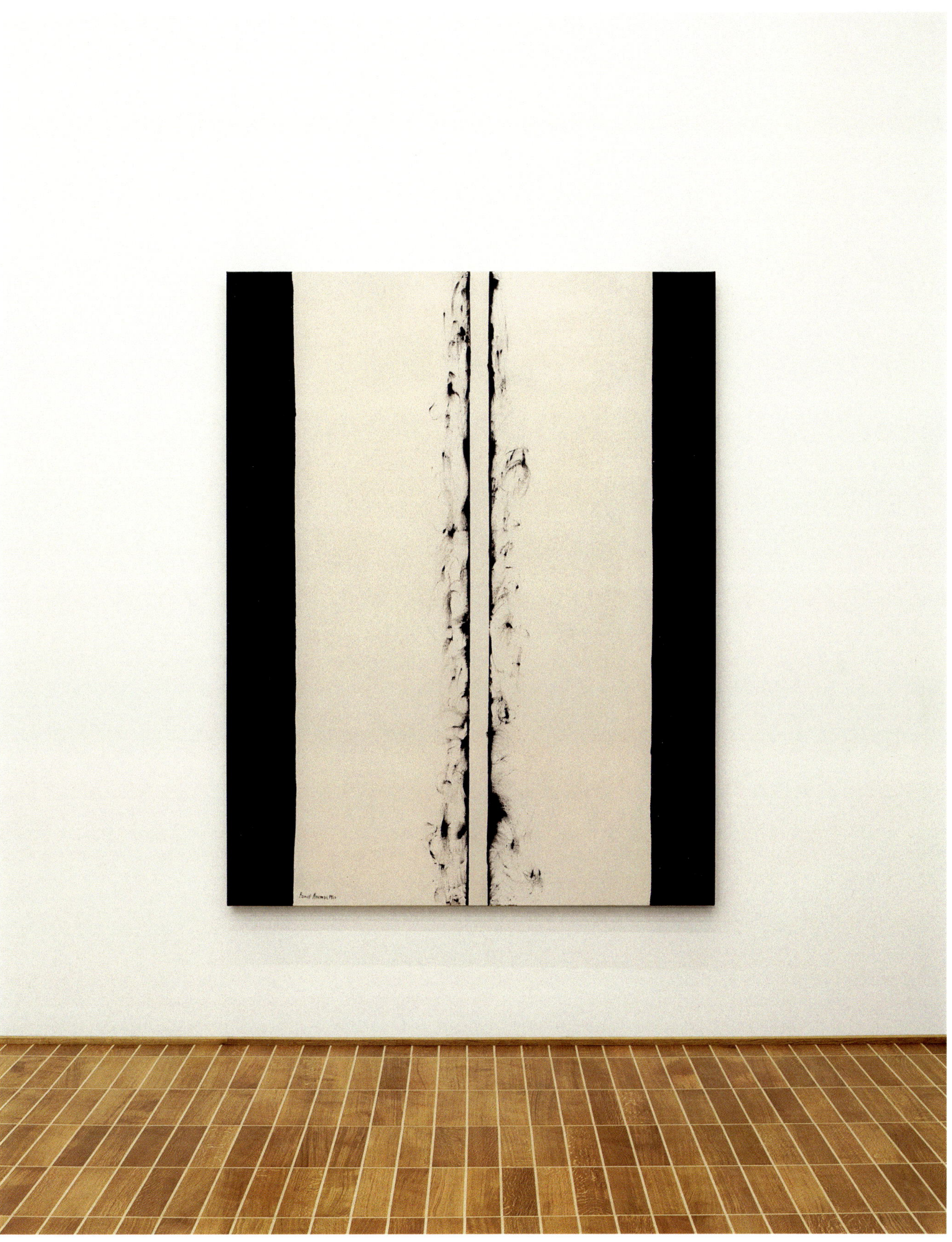

Barnett Newman, *White Fire II*, 1960

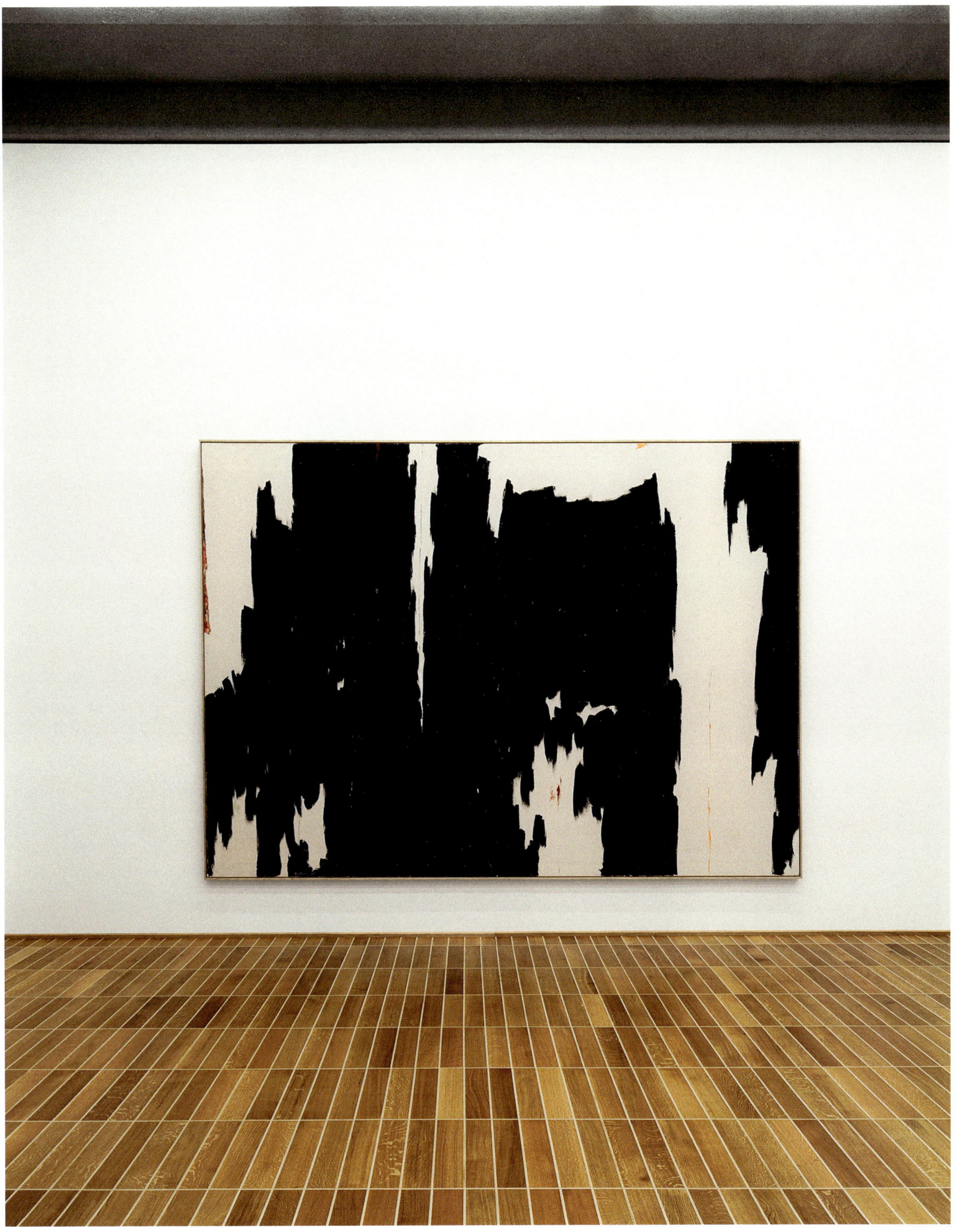

Clyfford Still, *1957—D No. 2*, 1957

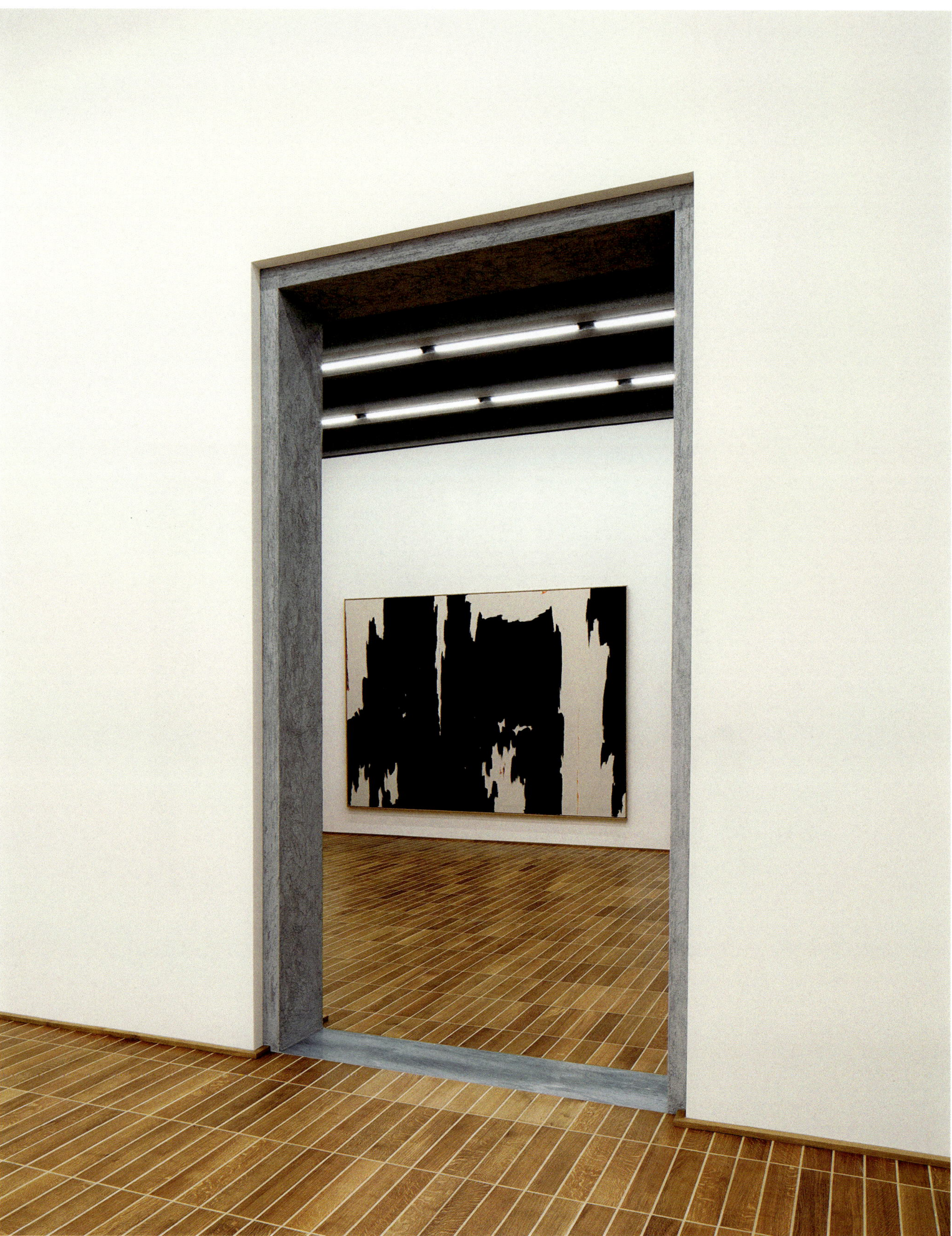

Barnett Newman, *Day Before One*, 1951

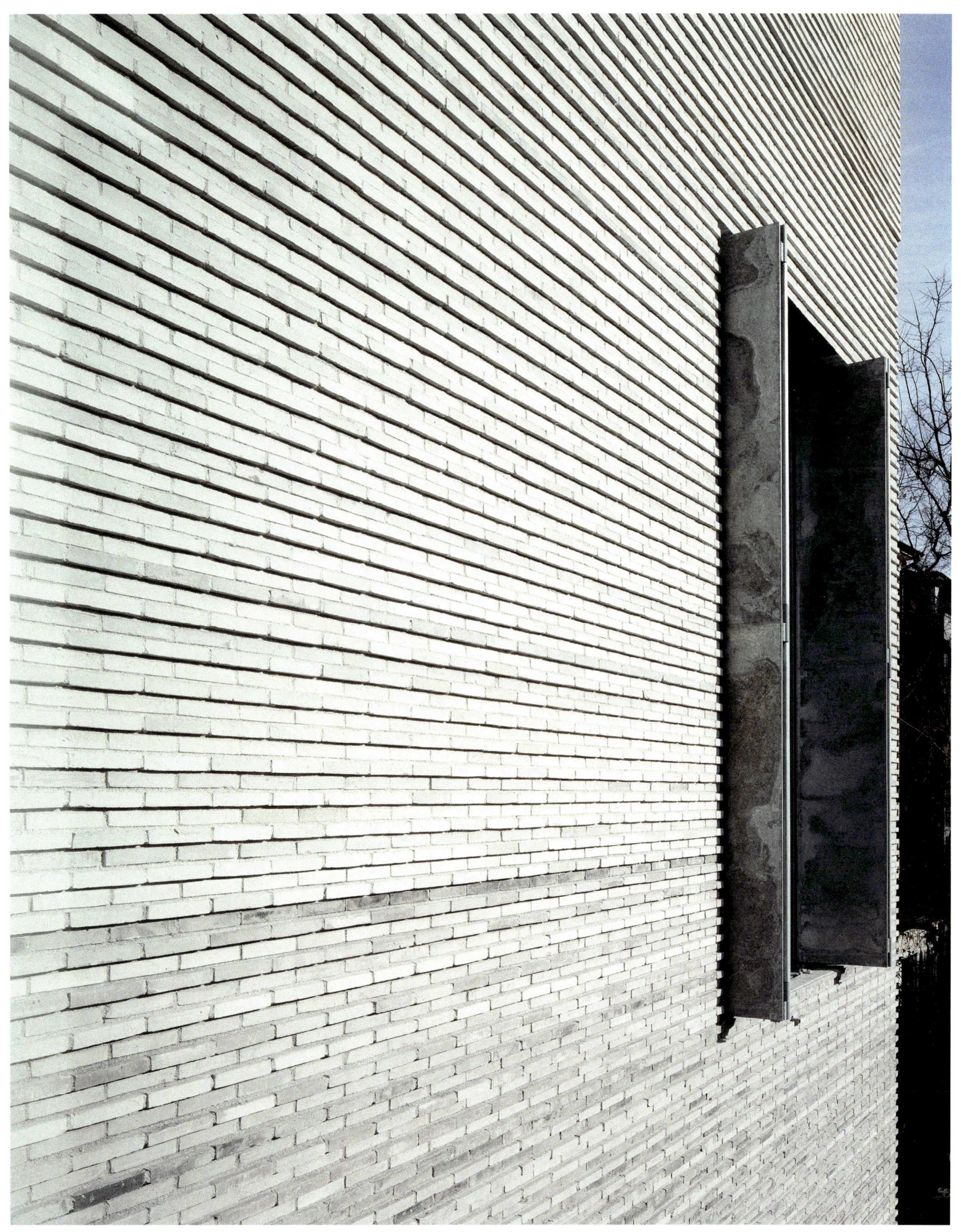

South facade with view into small courtyard; galvanized steel shutters

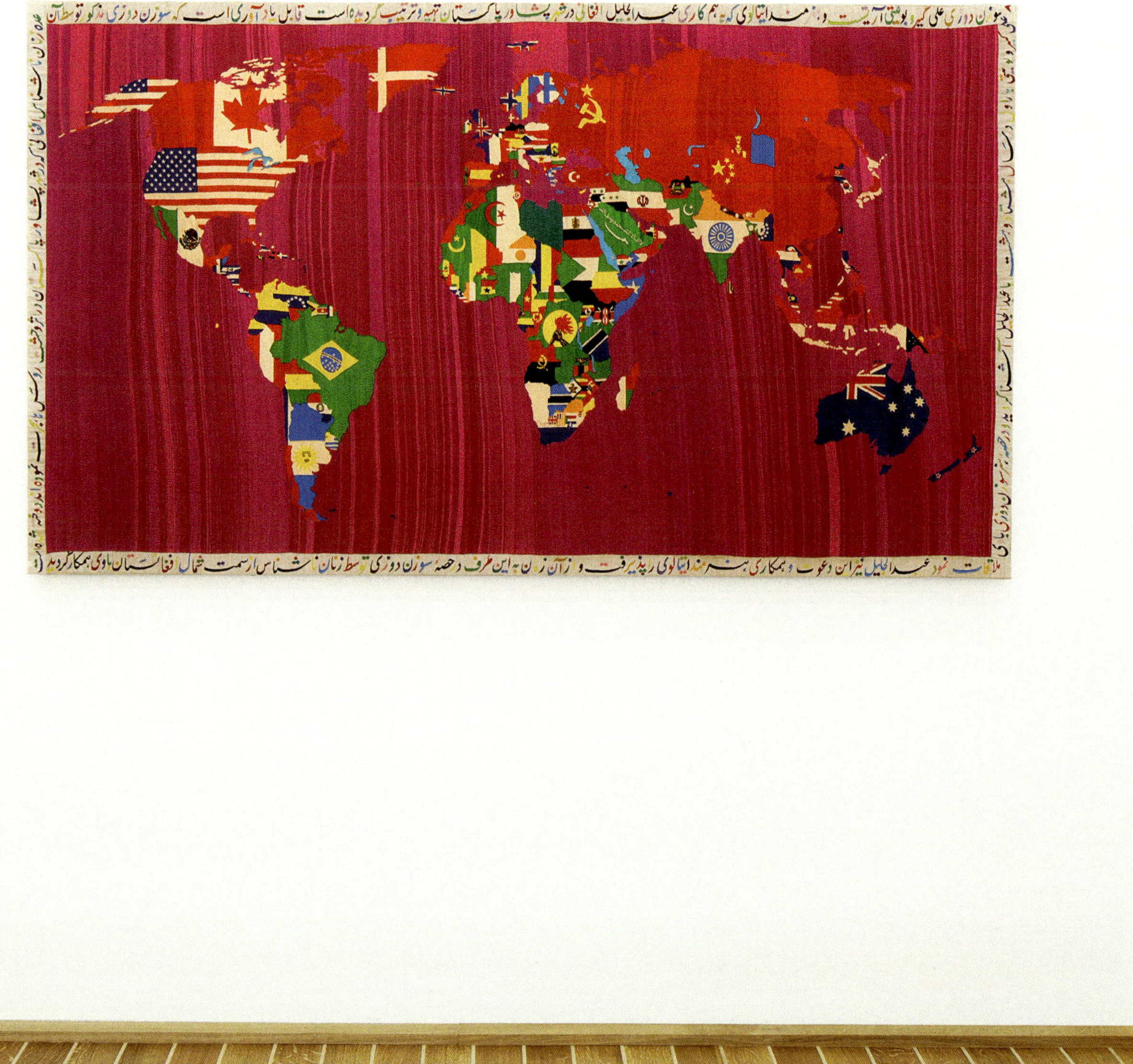

Alighiero Boetti, *Mappa*, 1988

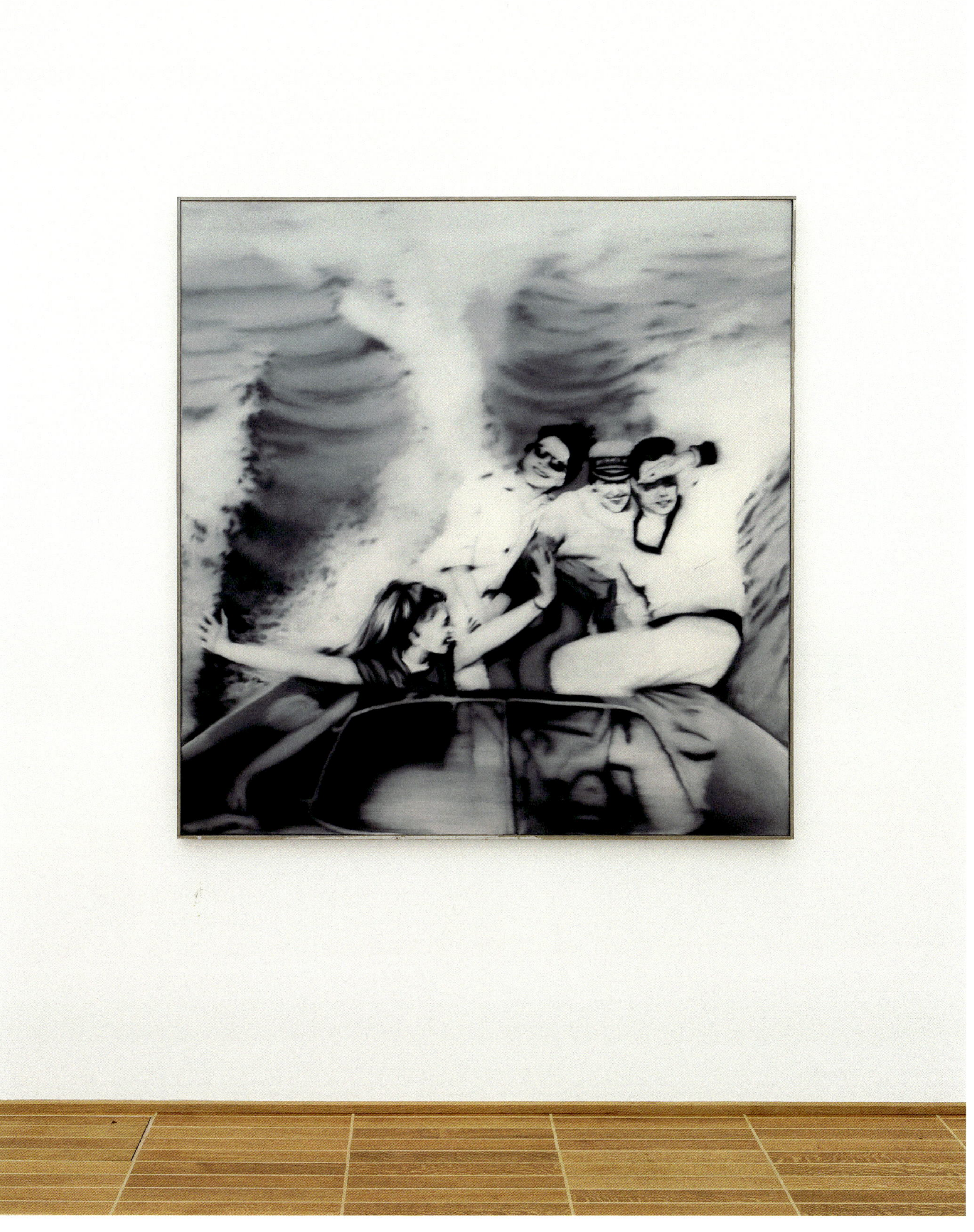

Gerhard Richter, *Motorboot* (Motorboat), 1965

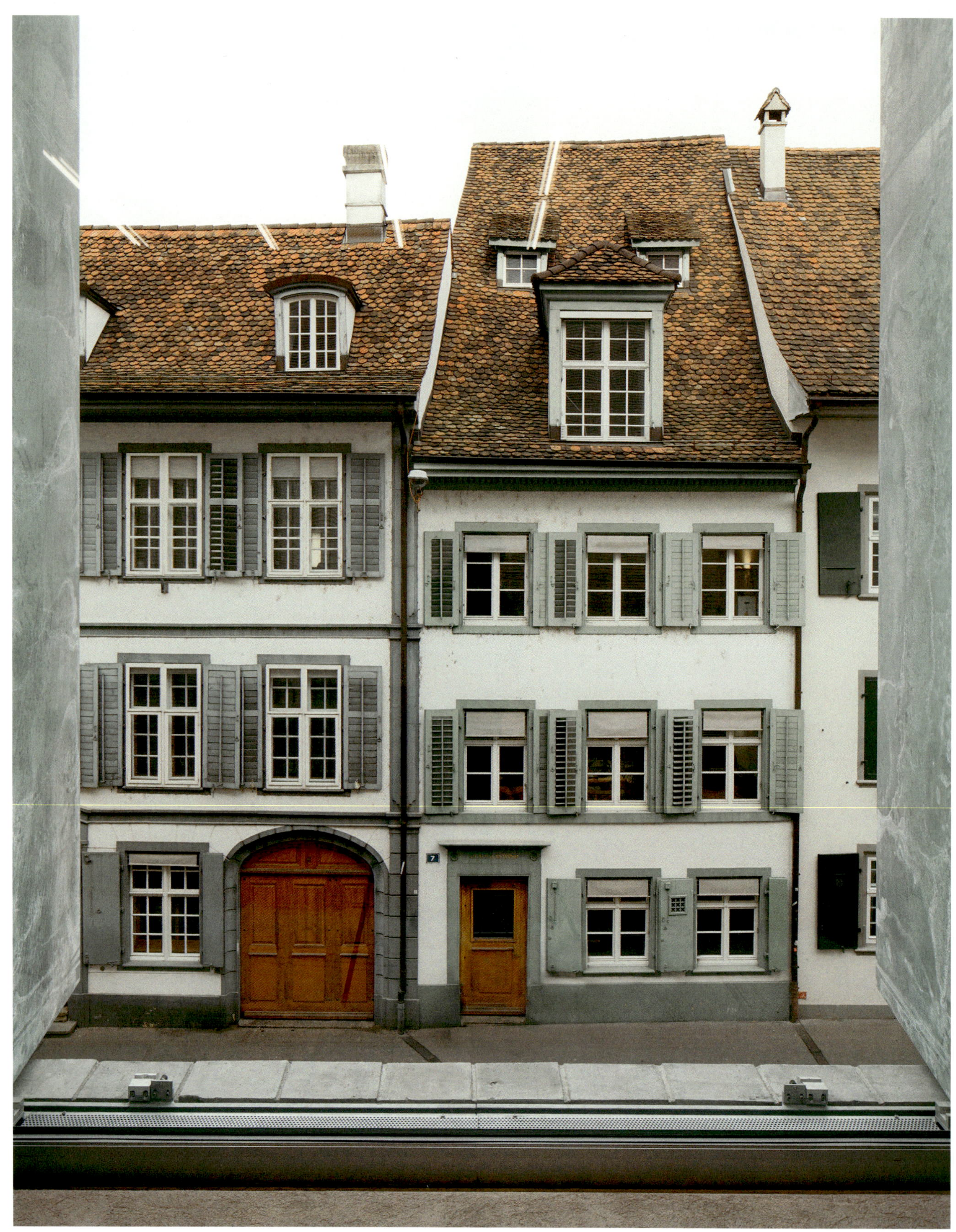

View of St. Alban-Vorstadt from the first floor

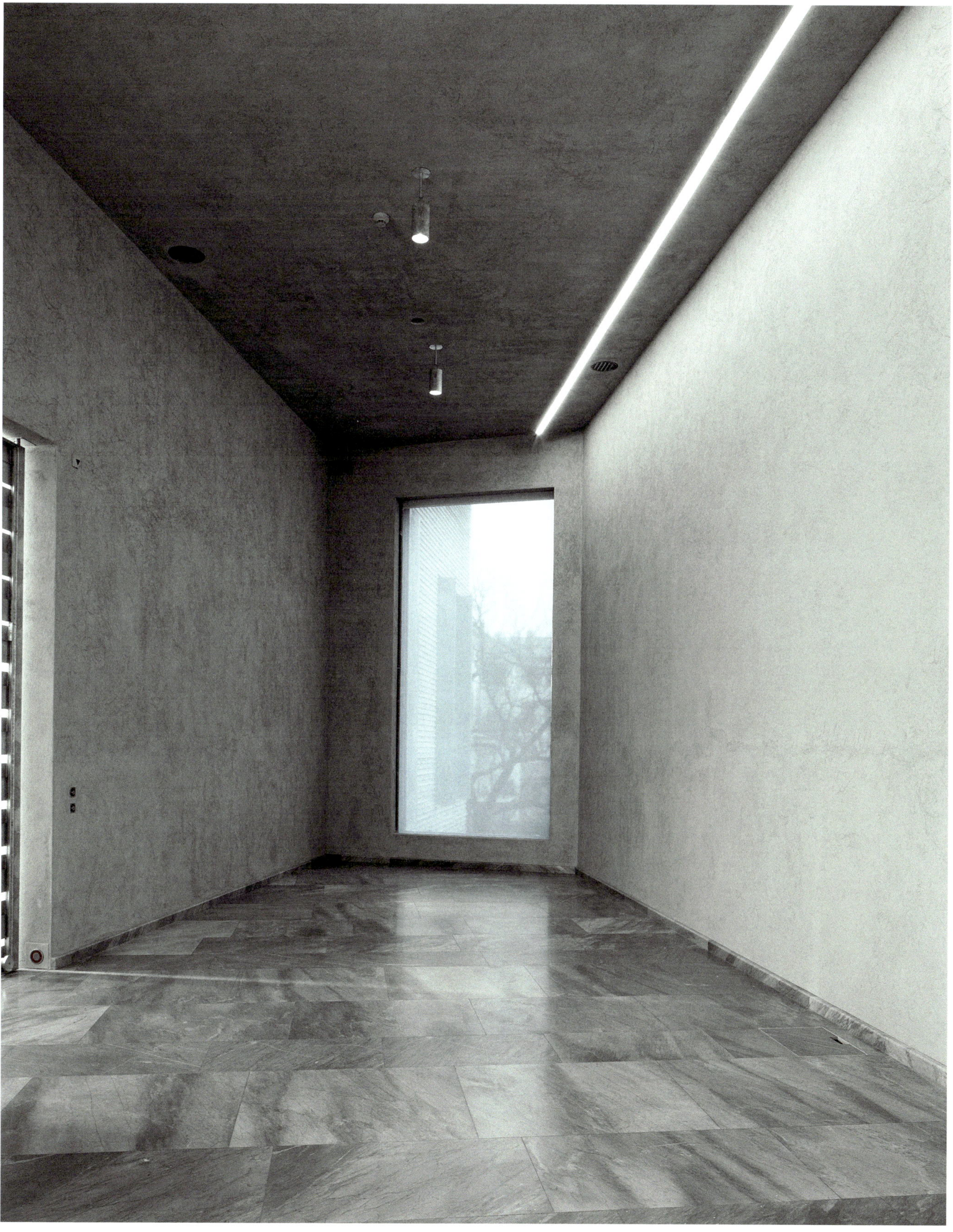

First-floor space 1.5

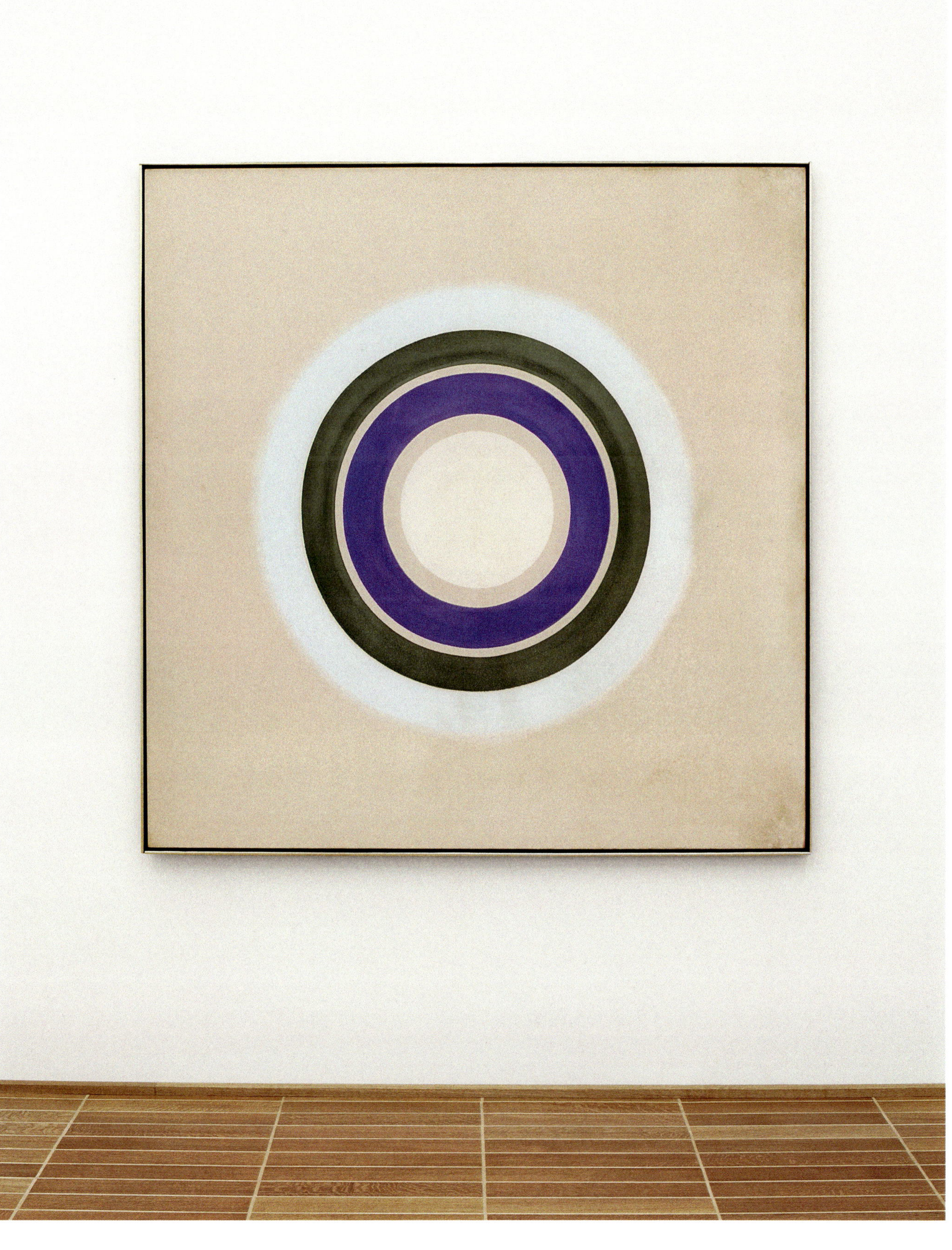

Kenneth Noland, *Winter Sun*, 1962, Emanuel Hoffmann Foundation, on permanent loan to the Öffentliche Kunstsammlung Basel

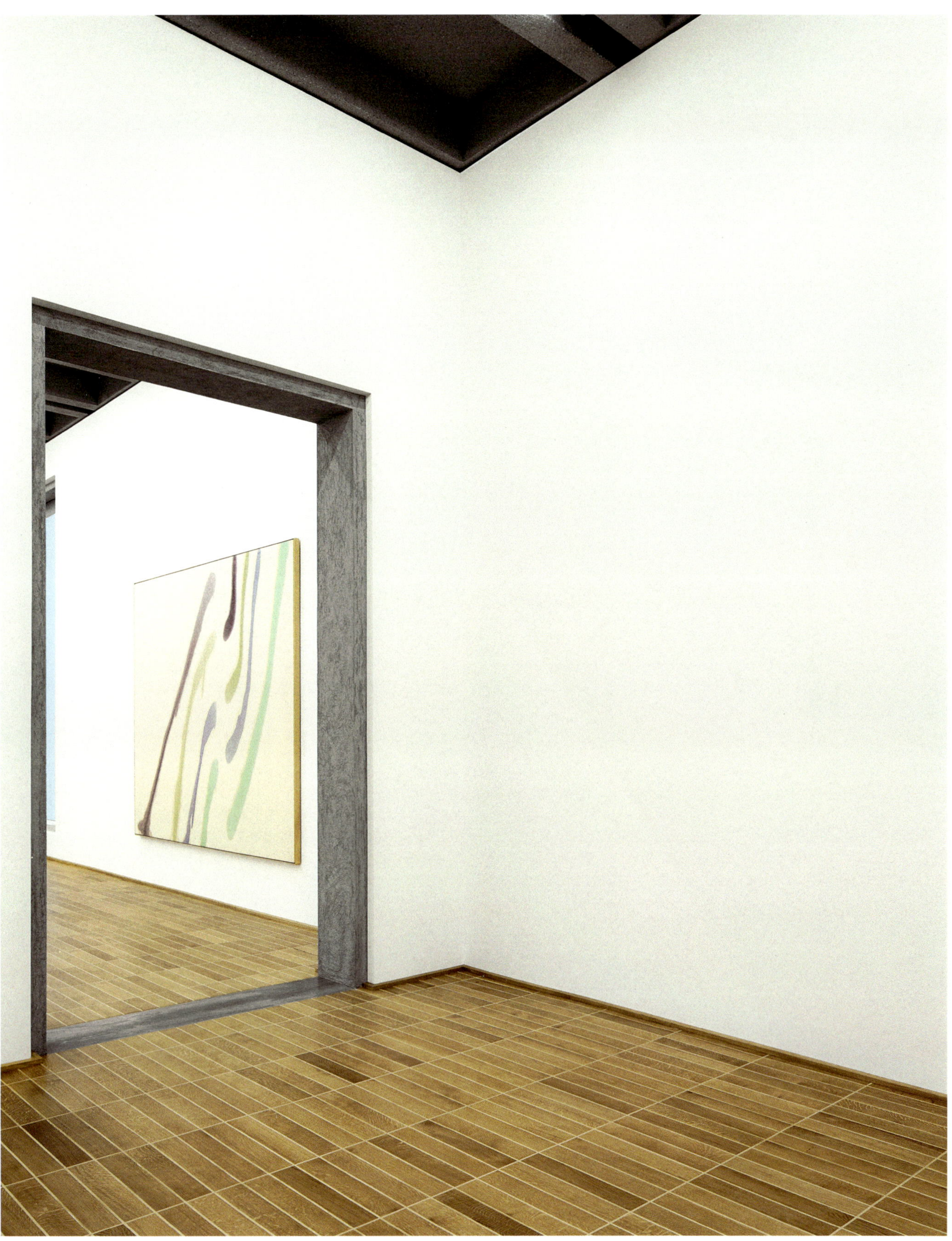

Morris Louis, *Delta Khi*, 1960

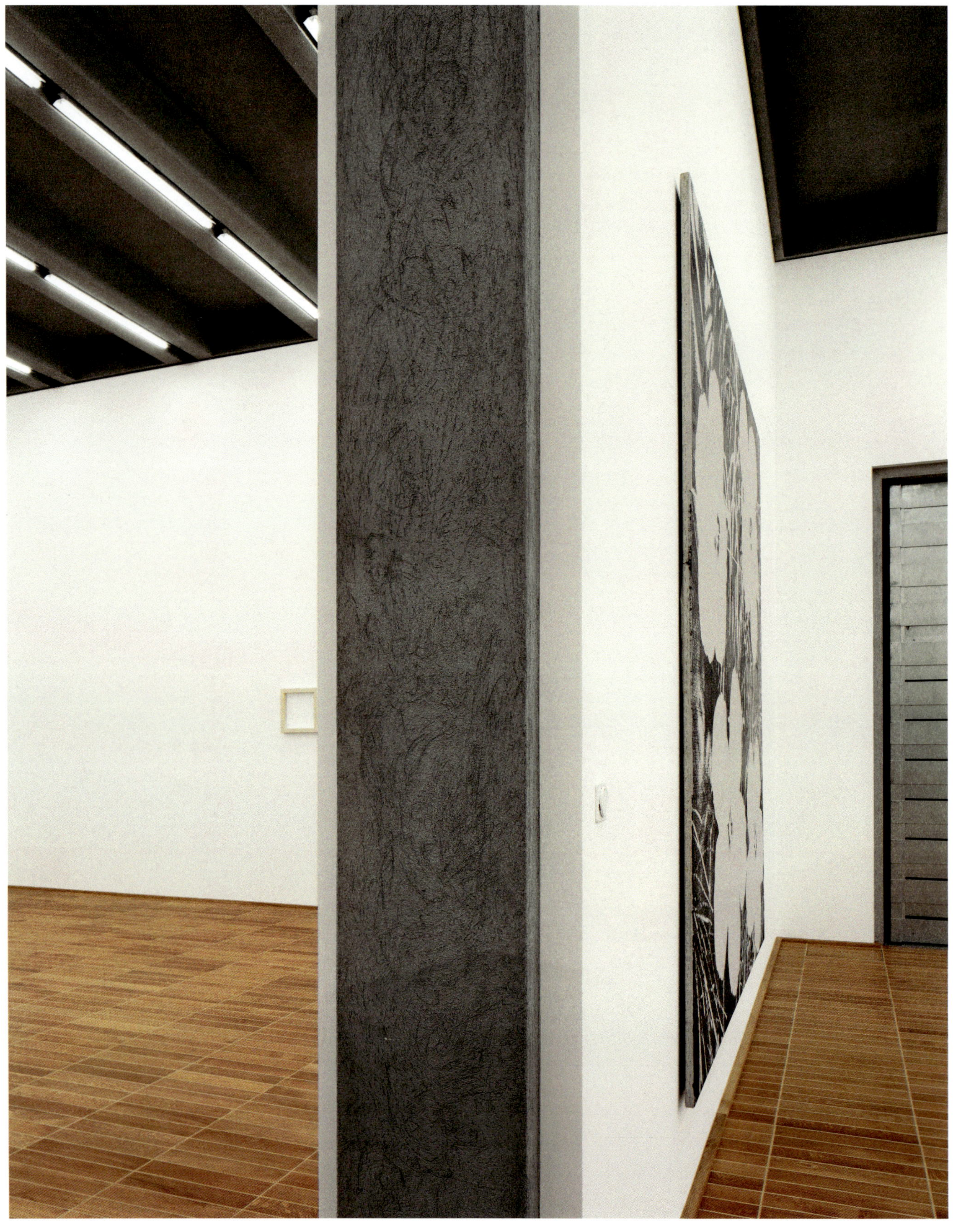

Sol LeWitt, *Wall Structure 5 4 3 2 1*, 1966–1973 (detail); Andy Warhol, *Ten-Foot Flowers*, 1967/68

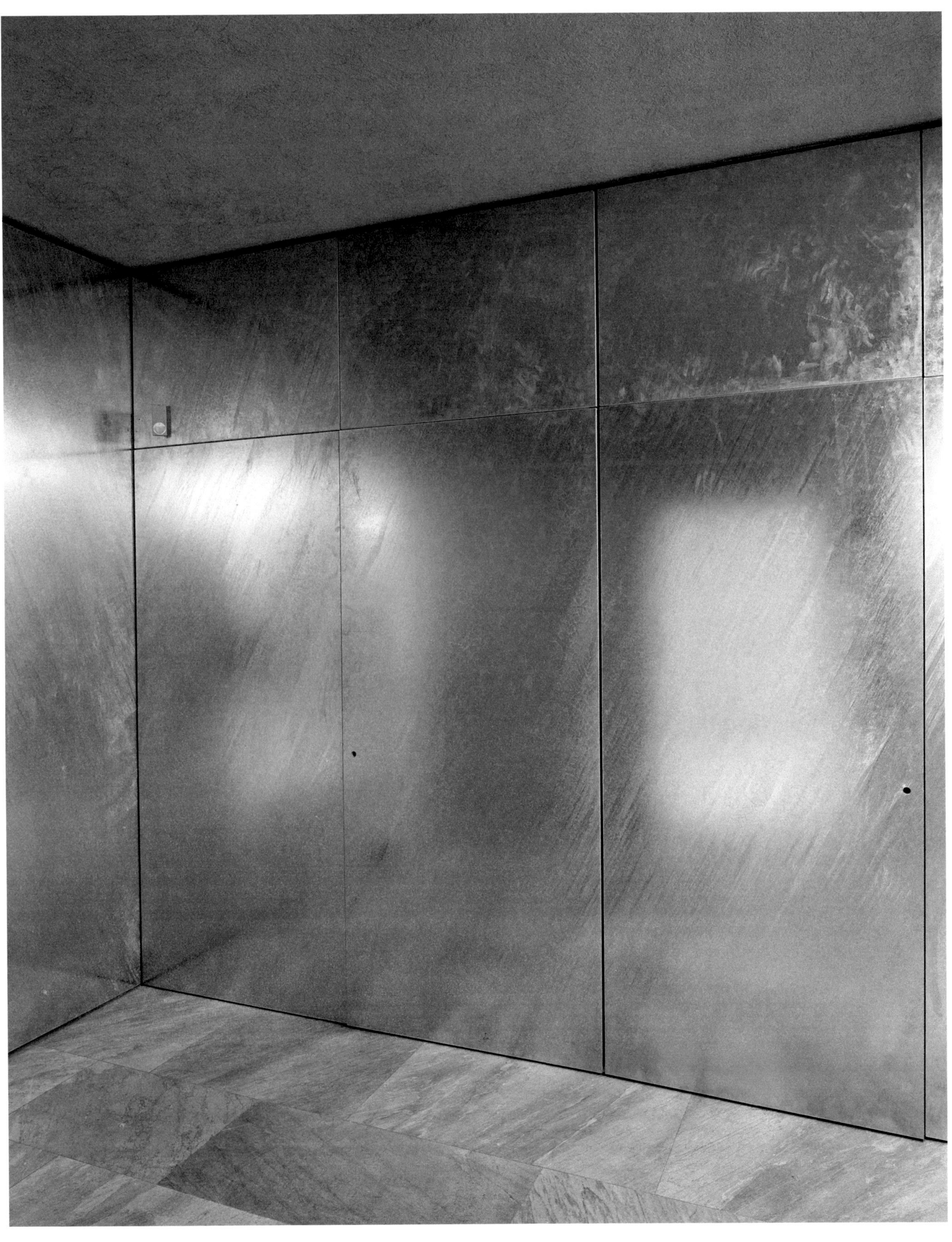

Elevator forecourt with marble floor, galvanized steel clad walls, galvanized steel clad doors, and scraped plaster ceiling

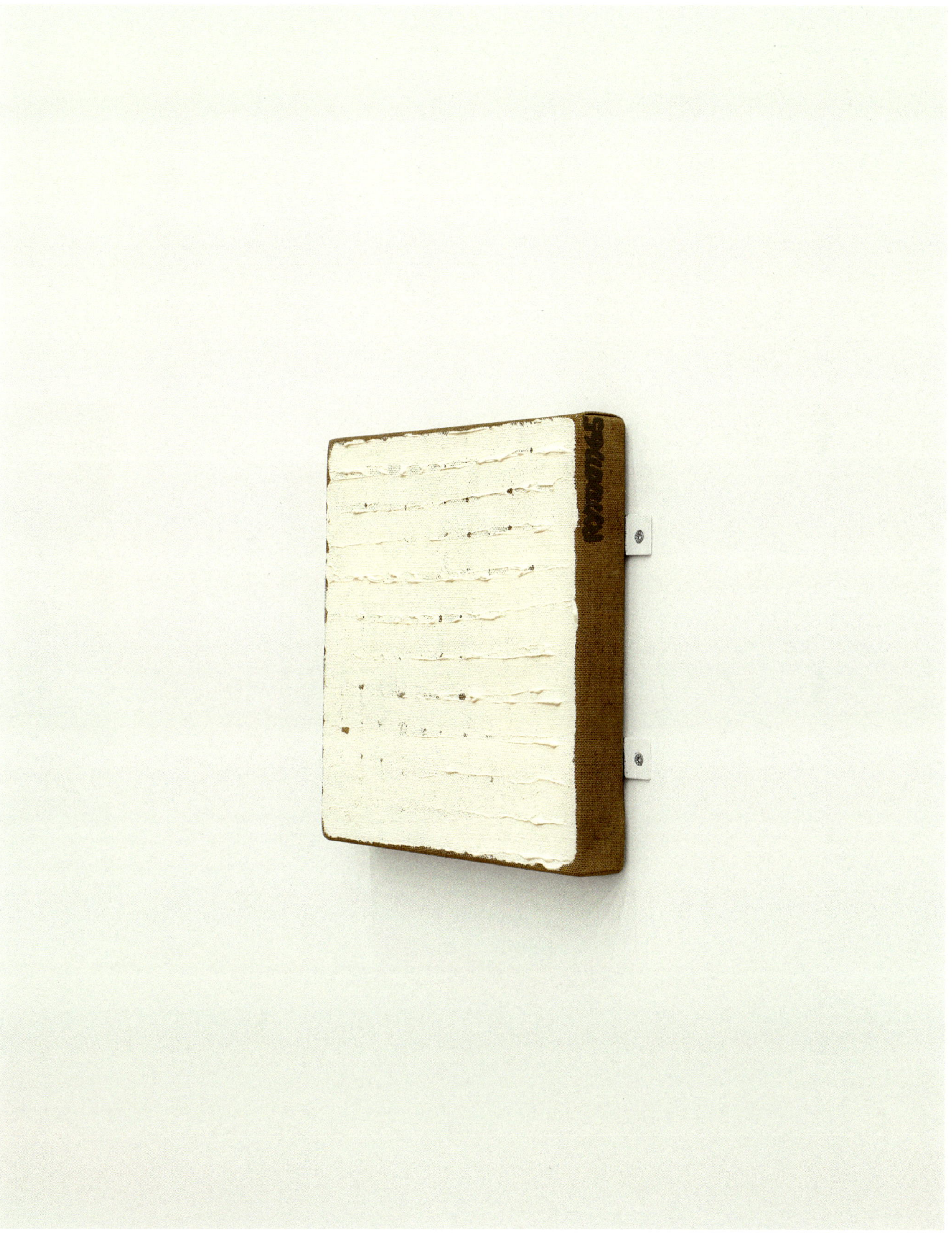

Robert Ryman, *Untitled*, 1965

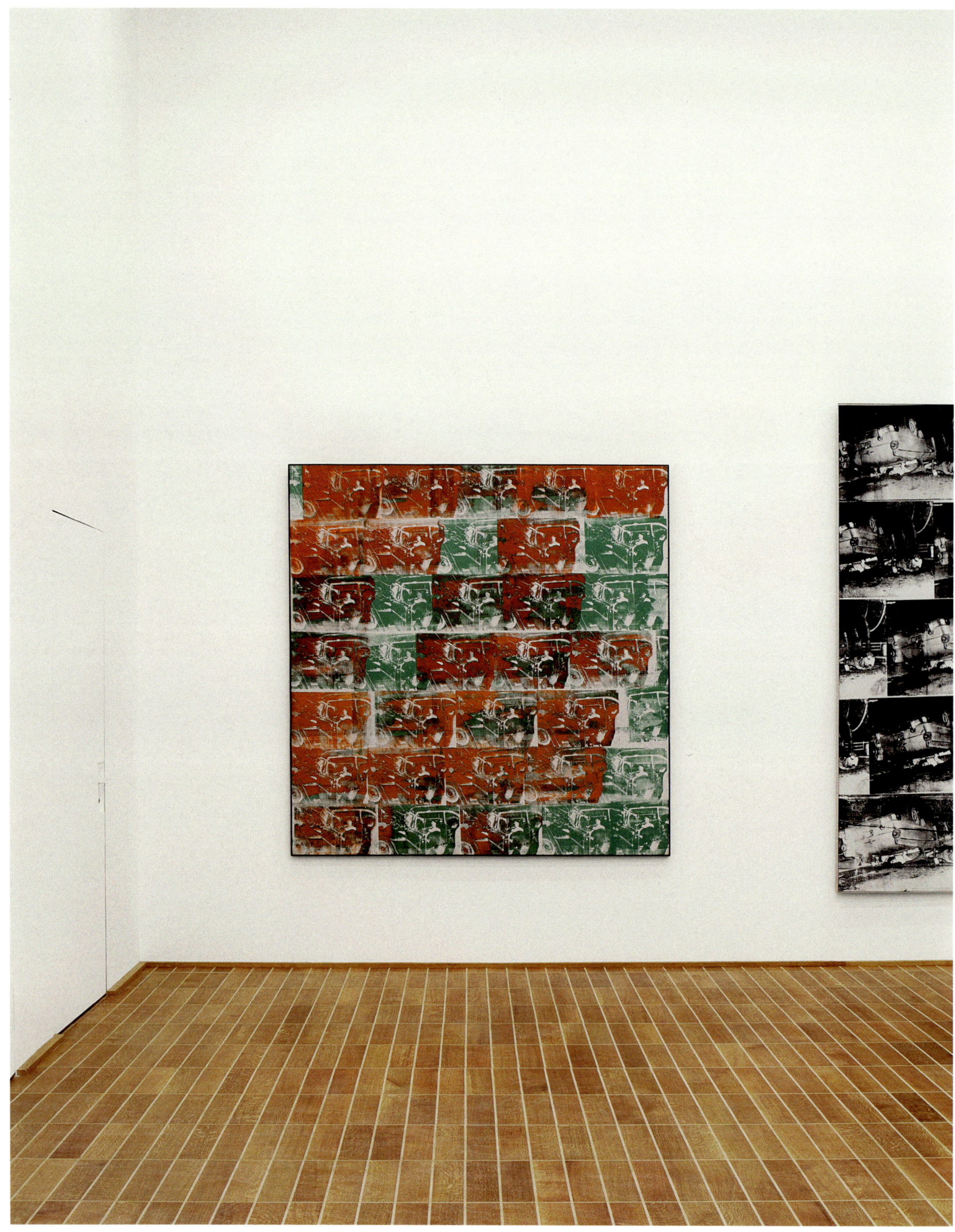

Andy Warhol, *Optical Car Crash*, 1962

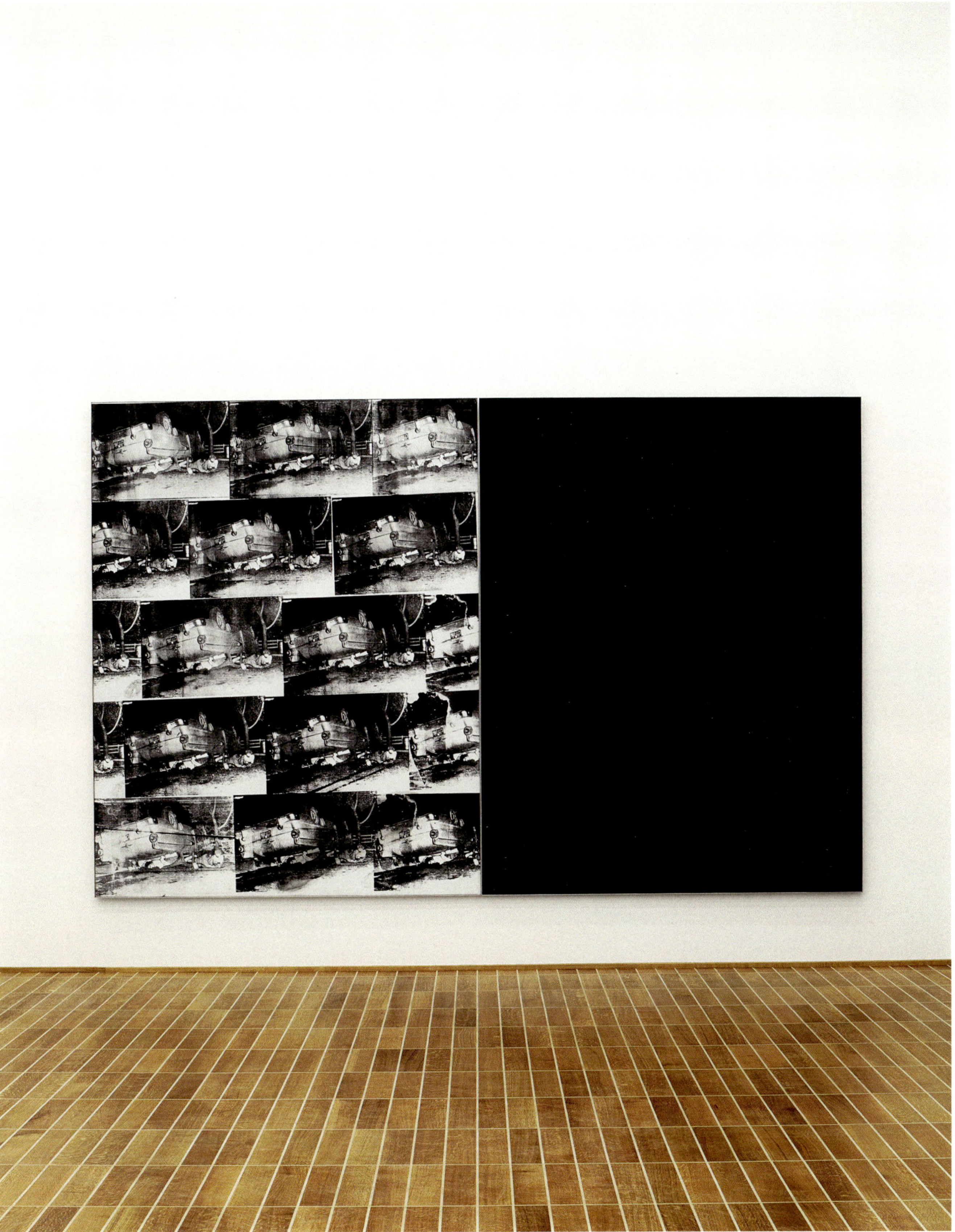

Andy Warhol, *Black and White Disaster #4*, 1963

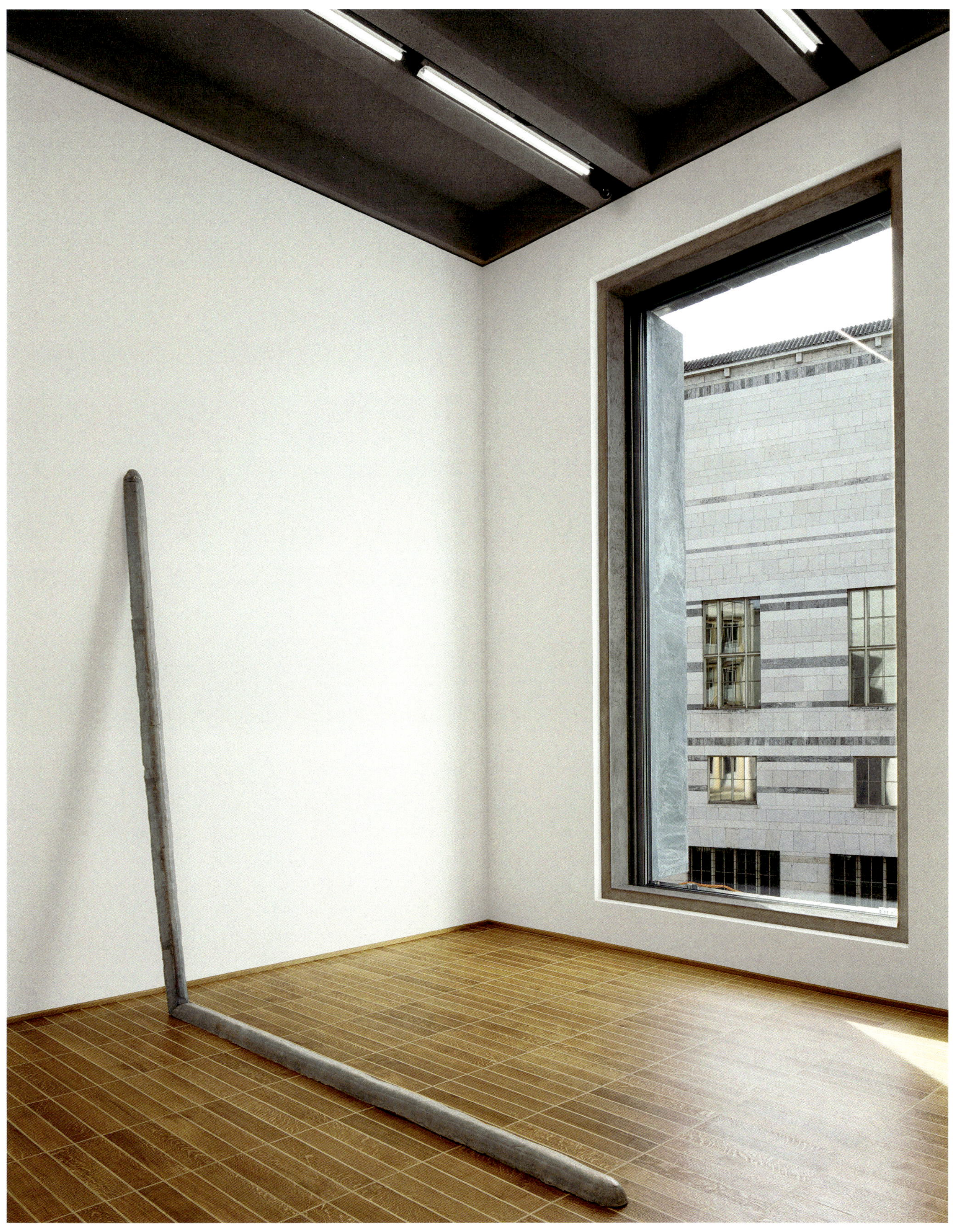

Bruce Nauman, *Untitled*, 1965, with view onto the main building

The Interaction of Art and Architecture
On the Content of the New Building

Bernhard Mendes Bürgi

What makes the Kunstmuseum Basel so unique—its salient characteristic, as it were—is the extraordinary breadth of its collection, which, with works of the very highest quality, spans the period from the fifteenth century to the present day, and is continuously updated. Assembling seven centuries of (Western) art history under one roof is no mean feat, especially as many of the great collections of old masters—that of the Museo Nacional del Prado in Madrid and the Musée du Louvre in Paris, for example—remain relatively static, having added little that postdates the end of the nineteenth century. And while The Museum of Modern Art in New York has indeed become a benchmark for modern and contemporary art, it does not have the echoing chamber of a collection of Old Masters, as the Kunstmuseum Basel does.

A steadily growing collection and ever more exacting demands with regard to how works of art are presented have repeatedly necessitated new architectural departures. The Kunstmuseum's main building on St. Alban-Graben designed by Christ & Bonatz in 1936 was therefore modernized in parallel to work on the new building. Earlier efforts to enlarge our architectural infrastructure culminated in the erection in 1980 of one of the world's first museums of contemporary art on St. Alban-Rheinweg, an annex that was likewise renovated in 2005. Since the acquisition of the adjoining Laurenz Building, moreover, premises formerly occupied by the Swiss National Bank, it has been able to house not only its library and offices there, but also the University of Basel's Art History Department. There were net gains in exhibition space in the main building too, and room enough for the installation of a bookstore / museum shop and bistro.

Recent years have seen not only a steady stream of acquisitions, especially of contemporary art, but also an intensification of our exhibition activities with major shows of Hans Holbein the Younger, Pablo Picasso, and, most recently, Charles Ray—to name but a few. Each of these exhibitions grew out of a different part of the collection (contemporary art, Modernism, and Old Masters) and each set out to investigate or revisit important aspects of the collection. As there were no plans to hold major exhibitions at the Kunstmuseum initially, the 1936 Christ & Bonatz building was not furnished with the necessary wherewithal in terms of infrastructure. Curators were therefore obliged to improvise, which they did by temporarily repurposing the galleries earmarked for the permanent collection. Not only did this necessitate many ad hoc rehangings, but it also had the effect of decimating the second-floor galleries and gravely impairing the unparalleled tour of Modernism that they might otherwise offer. Thus it really was our commitment to special exhibitions, coupled with our anxiety to spare the galleries reserved for the collection the upheavals that such shows are wont to cause, that triggered the search for a suitable premises close to the existing museum in which to install a dedicated exhibition infrastructure.

Above and beyond this, we wanted the new building to provide more space for an ever larger collection, especially for the works of the 1950s and later, such as those by Mark Rothko, Barnett Newman, Jasper Johns, Andy Warhol, and Donald Judd. This in turn would free up space in the main building for a collection ranging from Konrad Witz and Hans Holbein the Younger to Pablo Picasso and Alberto Giacometti, while the Museum für Gegenwartskunst (now the Kunstmuseum Basel | Gegenwart) would be able to focus exclusively on art from the 1990s to the present.

The creation of additional in situ storage space, first and foremost a specially air-conditioned area to be set aside for the photography collection that has grown considerably in recent years, was also high up on our wish list. From the logistical point of view, the closure of our satellite storage premises promised advantages that museums in big cities, which find themselves having to move their vaults further and further out of town, cannot usually enjoy. The Louvre's choice of Liévin near Lens for conservation and storage is but one example among many. Also essential was a loading bay for the delivery and dispatch of works of art in compliance with international standards, which in concrete terms meant a secure, air-conditioned drive-in loading bay with direct access to a cargo elevator. The other factors included visitor-friendly ticketing and cloakroom services and multipurpose event spaces. A large foyer with room for up to a thousand people that could be used for openings, symposia, performances, concerts, and lectures was considered especially desirable. Nor should space for the museum's educational and outreach activities be forgotten.

If at all possible, the new building was to be situated in the immediate vicinity of the main building, thus becoming an integral, and indeed assertive, part of its specific urban context. The idea was that it should enter into a dialogue with the main building; not to outshine it, but to enhance and empower it.

The main stipulations of the concept, therefore, were that the galleries be centrally located, that the architecture in the exhibition areas support rather than dominate the art, and that the main and the new buildings be physically connected. The overriding aim was to upgrade the infrastructure of the Kunstmuseum Basel as custodian of a world-famous collection, and to strike a balance between our collecting and exhibiting activities. The new building was also to become an architectural landmark, symbolizing an innovative new departure both for Basel as a city and for museums worldwide.

THE REALIZATION

Once the Burghof site had been purchased, we were able to invite entries to an anonymous competition for the building to be erected there. The design selected was that submitted by Christ & Gantenbein, a comparatively young architects' office from Basel, which is perhaps surprising given the many famous names that took part. The winning project submitted in the second stage of the selection process already bore all the distinctive hallmarks that were to be developed as planning progressed, above all the concave "kink" that references a historical group of houses, and lends an exterior presence that might otherwise seem monolithic, a wonderful, almost playful lightness of touch. Then there is the LED frieze combining state-of-the-art IT with a traditional neoclassical frieze like the one that adorns the facade of the museum of 1849 by Melchior Berry on Augustinergasse, which for a long time housed the Öffentliche Kunstsammlung. Even the underpass connecting the two buildings beneath Dufourstrasse and lit with daylight from the courtyard at the rear was likewise an integral part of Christ & Gantenbein's plans right from the start.

As the planning work progressed, this underground passage on the first lower level acquired an ever sharper profile as a generously dimensioned access area far removed from conventional notions of tunnels as dark and narrow conduits. Thus it encompasses both a large foyer and, thanks to the daylight supplied by the aforementioned courtyard, the first of the exhibition spaces. Following the conceptual logic of the design, these are spread over all four of the floors that are open to the public, and actually monopolize the whole of the first and second floors. Despite featuring works by Frank Stella, among others, the foyer does not actually constitute an exhibition space as such. It is more an event space accentuated by works of art, which for a change of emphasis can be rehung from time to time. The underpass allows visitors to move freely between the main building and the extension, which can also be reached directly from the street via its own ground-floor entrance area. All the public access areas have the same matte gray marble flooring, which looks especially impressive in the monumental stairwell.

The stairwell, incidentally, is an exceptionally good example of Christ & Gantenbein's inspired engagement with the main building, as evidenced by their use of rough scraped plaster for parts of the walls and ceilings, and by the round skylight crowning the almost sculptural-looking staircase. The staircase provides access to the second floor which, furnished with skylights, is to be used mainly for special exhibitions. That these would draw on works from all parts of the collection was a point the architects should be reminded of, I felt. They should certainly not imagine that the only works that would ever hang there would be Modernist or later—works for which the proverbial white cube counts as the ideal space. Their job was rather to create a space that would make just as good a backdrop for the art of the Renaissance and of the seventeenth, eighteenth, and nineteenth centuries. The first-floor equivalent of the skylights that were a *conditio sine qua non* of the second floor are the tall windows built into the side walls which, besides flooding the galleries with light, also permit wonderful views across the city and lend vivid immediacy to the architectural presence of the main building across the street. The linear LED lighting is built into the concrete ribs in the ceiling, which, besides making for structural clarity, also accommodate the HVAC ducts.

All the galleries are perfectly proportioned in terms of length, breadth, and ceiling height—this being just as essential to the effective staging of art as the harmonious interaction of floor, ceiling, and wall. Both the architects and the museum attached the utmost importance to the physical, sensuous presence of the materials used for every detail, no matter how tiny, and discussed these at great length—whether or not there should be baseboards, for example, how the doorways between galleries should be articulated, what the metal fire doors and window shutters should look like. Even the thick layer of plaster coating the walls was chosen not just to facilitate the installation of the artworks, but also as an expression of our conviction that only in an exhibition architecture made of carefully selected materials can art truly flourish. The choice of industrial parquet flooring in the galleries deserves a special mention here. Once widely used, it has become quite rare in recent years, although its sensational reinterpretation at the hands of Christ & Gantenbein makes it once again contemporary. The quality materials on the inside are matched by the brick facades on the outside, which from ground up pass through several subtle gradations of gray.

To be able to achieve such physical presence and architectural rigor, one decision was clear right from the start: specifically, to dispense with the much-vaunted system of flexible room dividers so often used by many new museums, among them Renzo Piano's Whitney Museum of American Art in New York. Insisting on definitive walls rather than non-committal partitions requires great courage on the part of both museum and architects. But here, too, *unité de doctrine* prevailed—the doctrine being our shared determination to eschew the kind of faceless, nondescript, protean interiors that are currently en vogue. Besides, what makes the new building's exhibition spaces so attractive is the fact that they can be used with absolute flexibility. Nor are there any permanent installations in the pipeline that might stand in the way of a potential "reinvention" of the new building. The need to obtain orthogonal exhibition spaces from an irregularly shaped plot, which being relatively small had to be exploited to the full, was likewise an important factor informing the architects' design. Thus the galleries vary in size and in some cases are larger than those in the main building. Being arranged in sequences, moreover, they will allow us to create coherent exhibition organisms, which in their turn will function as germ cells for the vitality and radiance of the institution as a whole.

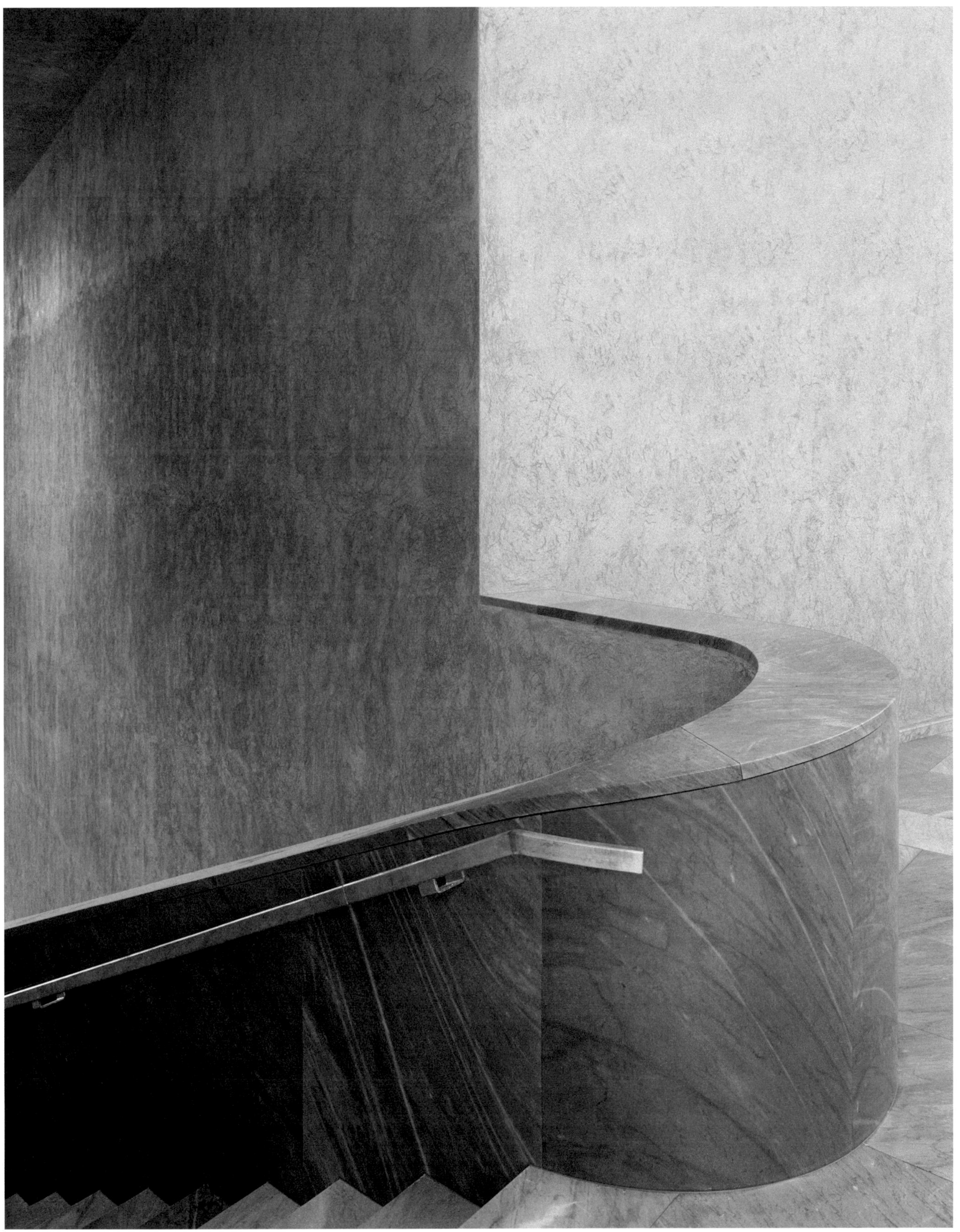

Second-floor landing

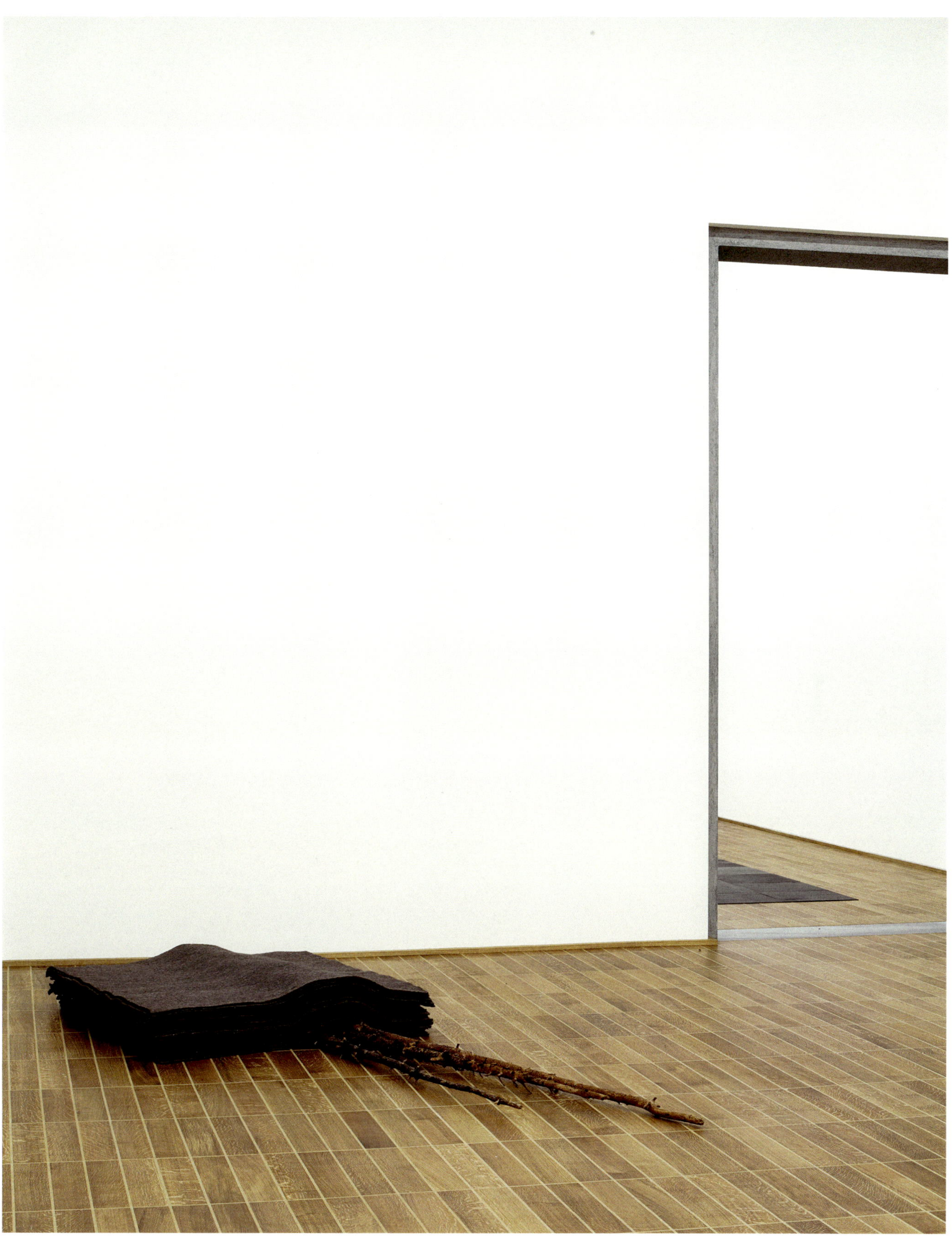

Joseph Beuys, *Schneefall* (Snowfall), 1965, Emanuel Hoffmann Foundation,
on permanent loan to the Öffentliche Kunstsammlung Basel

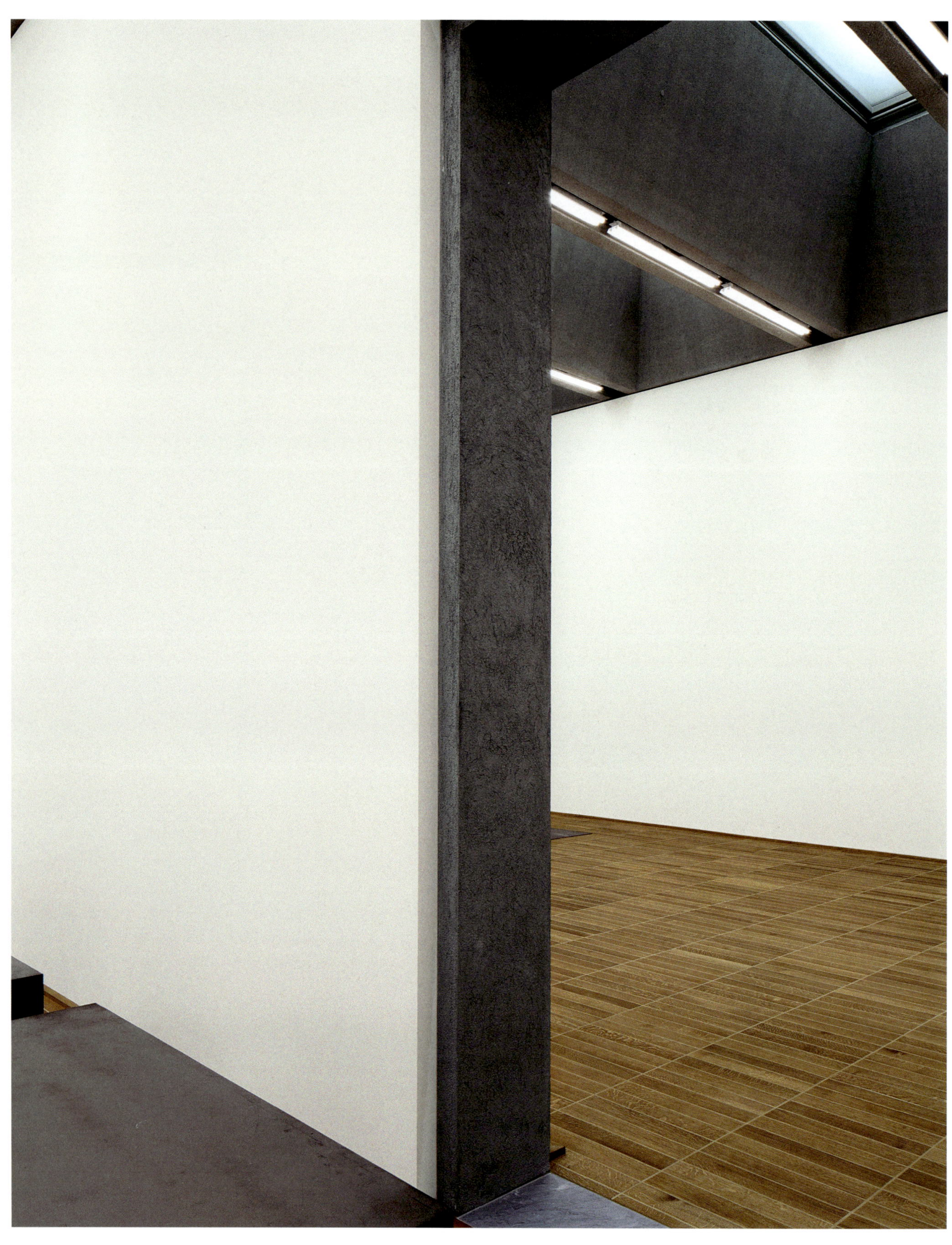

Second-floor galleries with oiled oak parquet with wood cement grouting, plasterboard walls, scraped plaster door frame with marble threshold, ceilings with concrete elements, LED lighting, and skylight

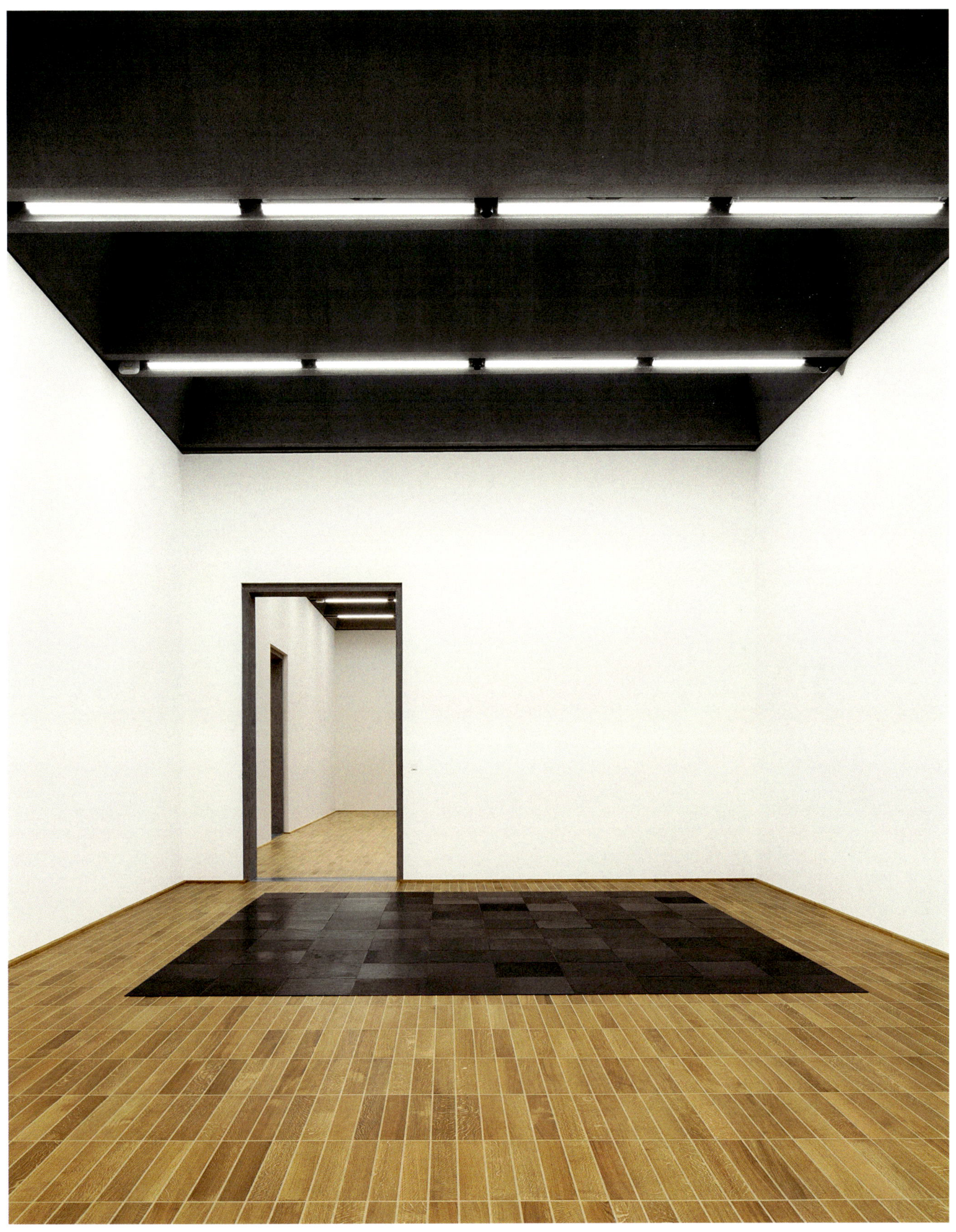

Carl Andre, *10 × 10 Altstadt Square*, 1967

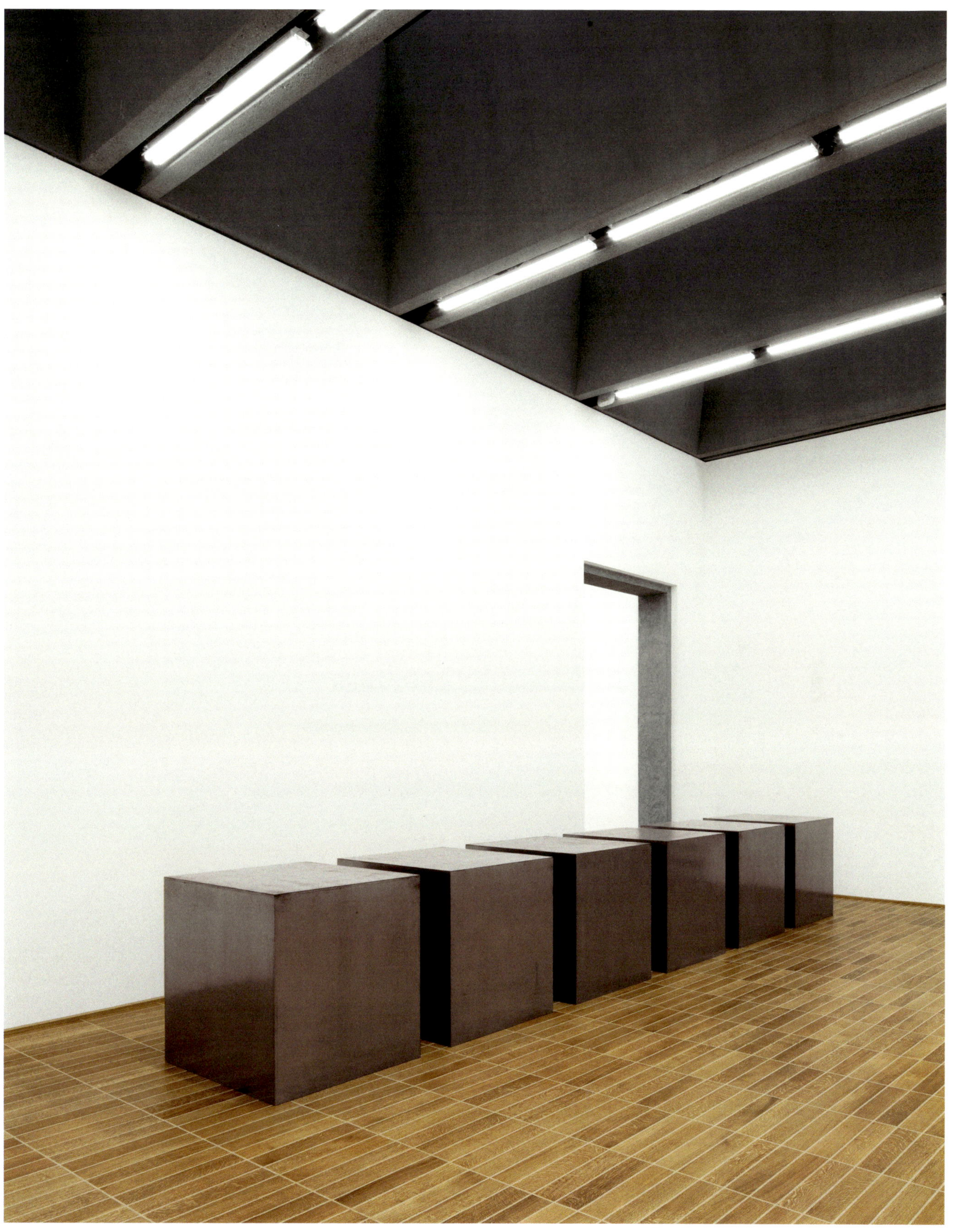

Donald Judd, *Untitled*, 1969

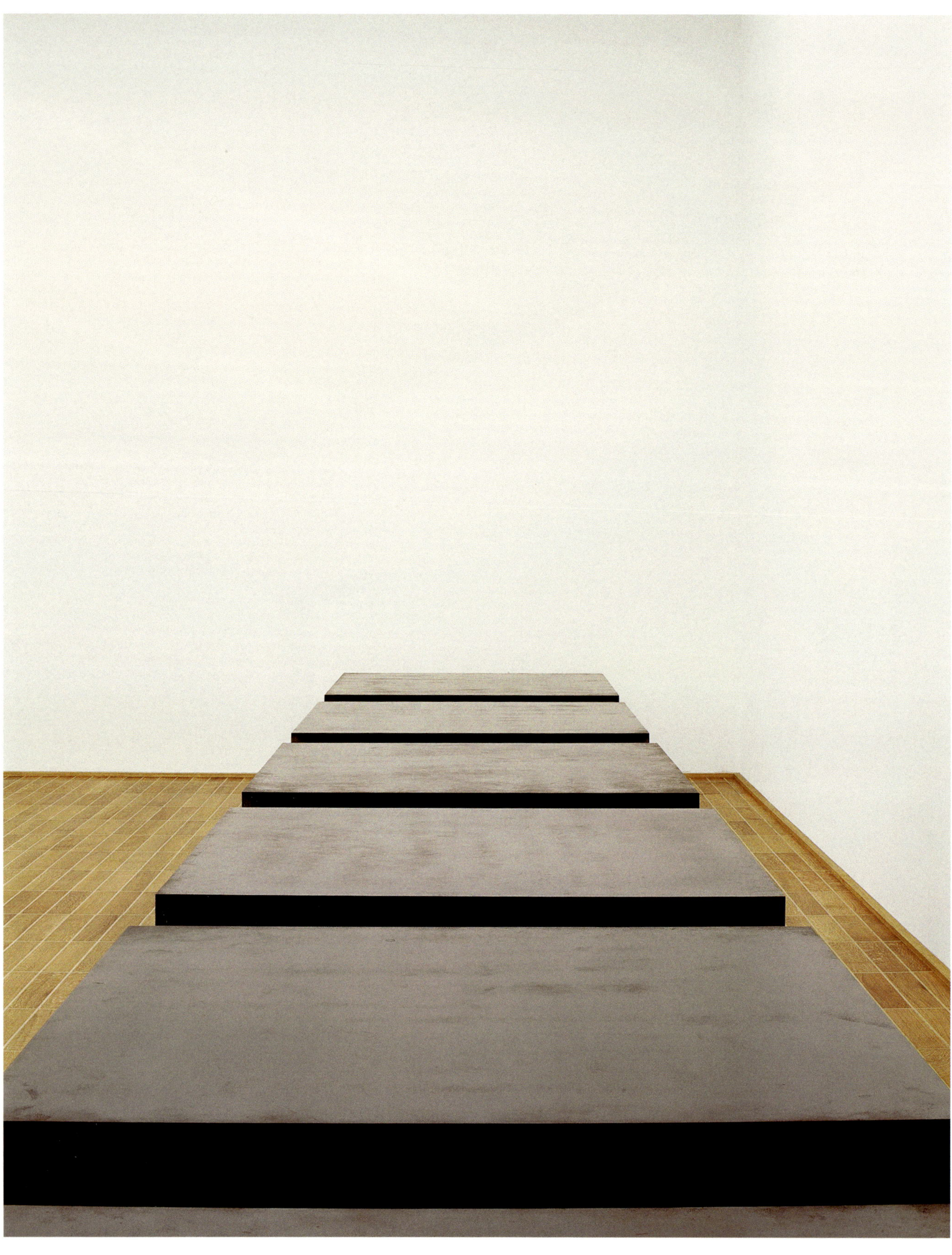

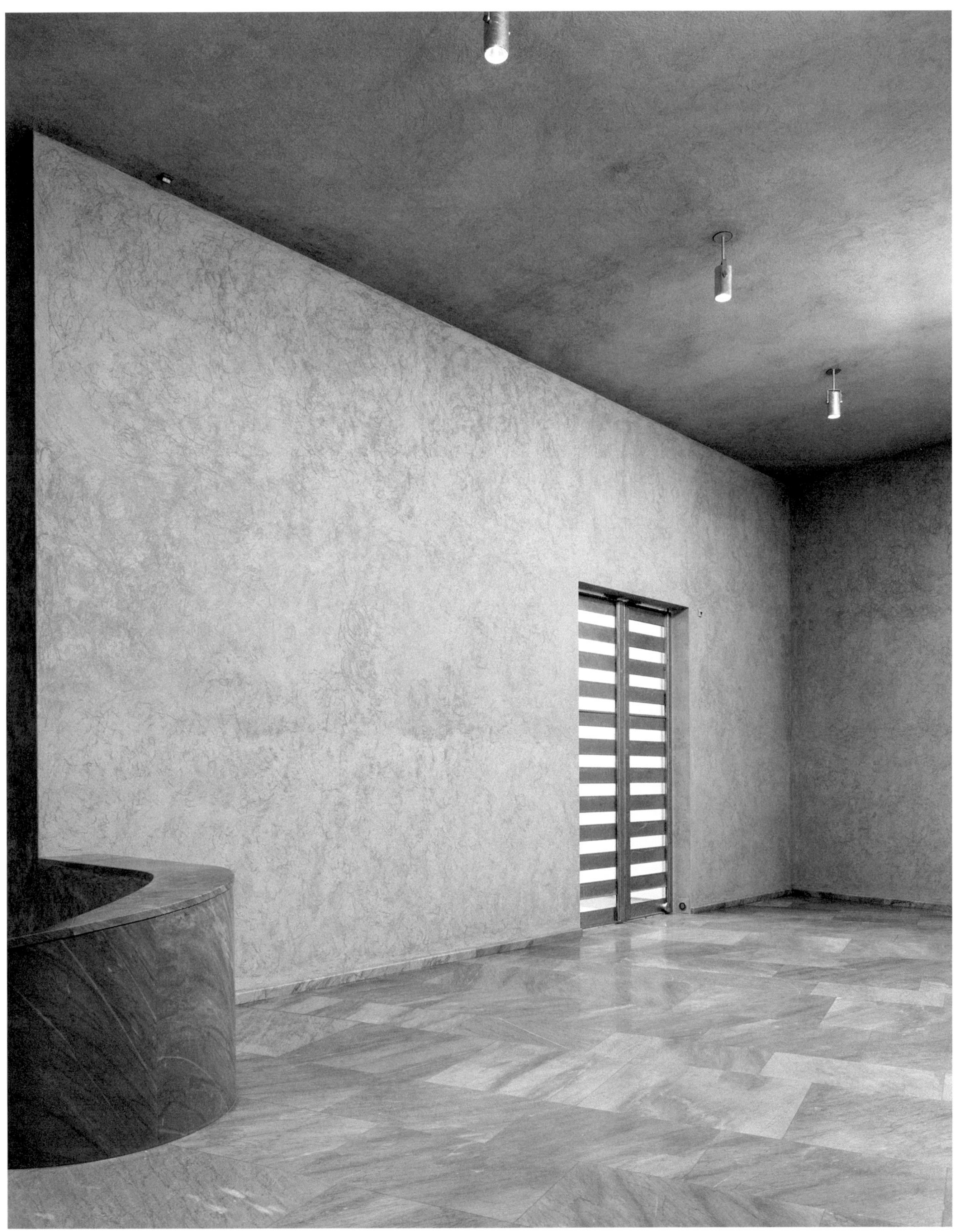

Second-floor landing

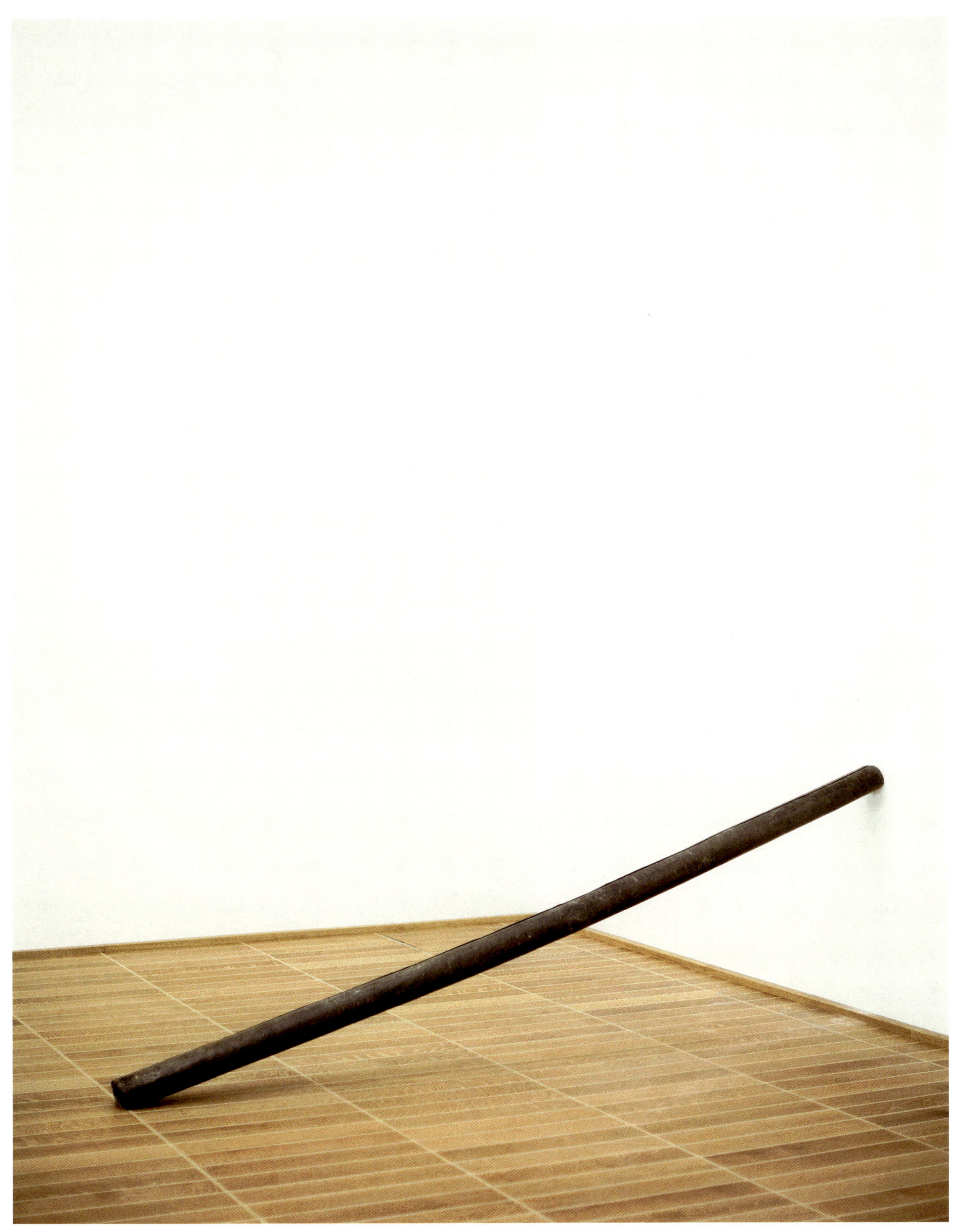

Richard Serra, *Pipe Prop*, 1969

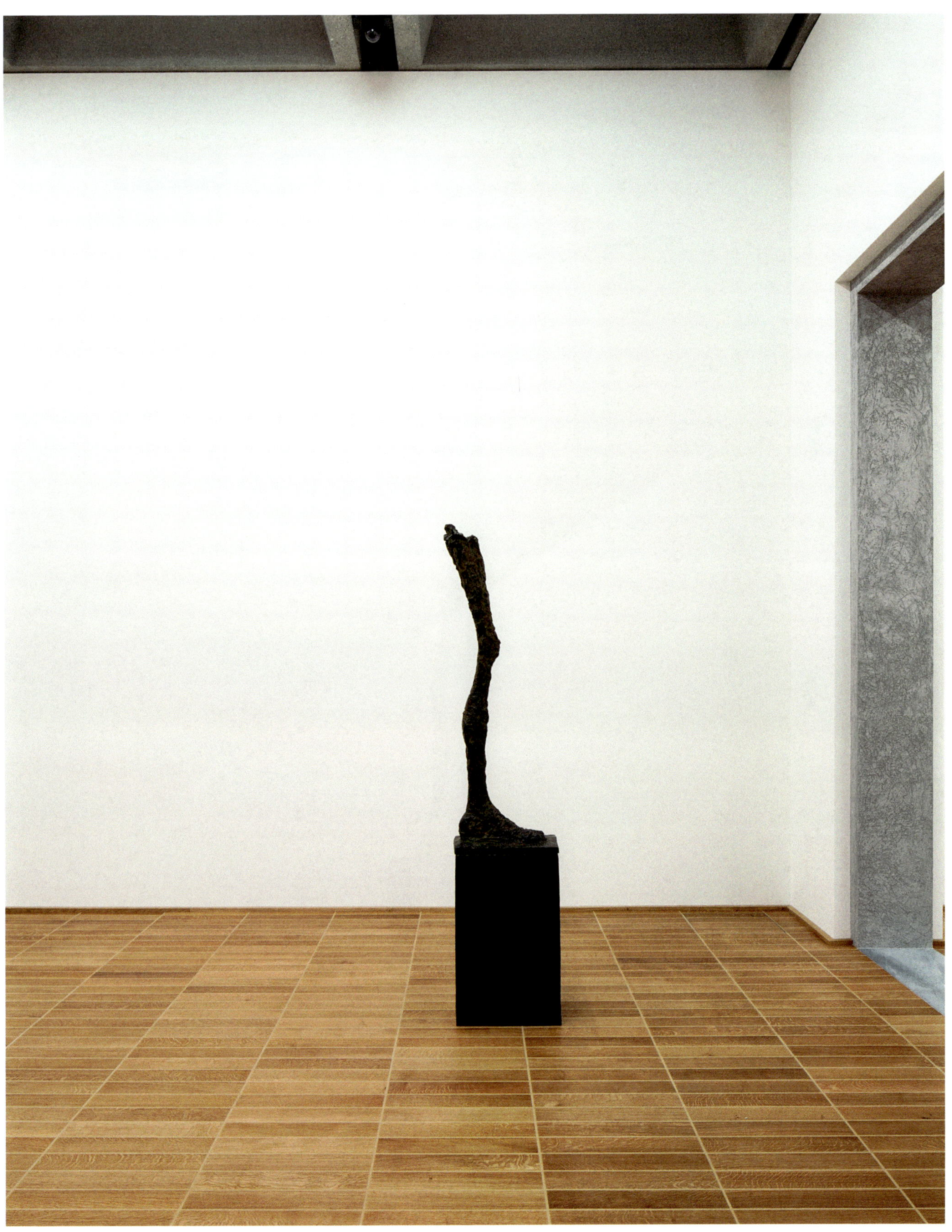

Alberto Giacometti, *La jambe*, 1958, on permanent loan from the Alberto Giacometti Foundation

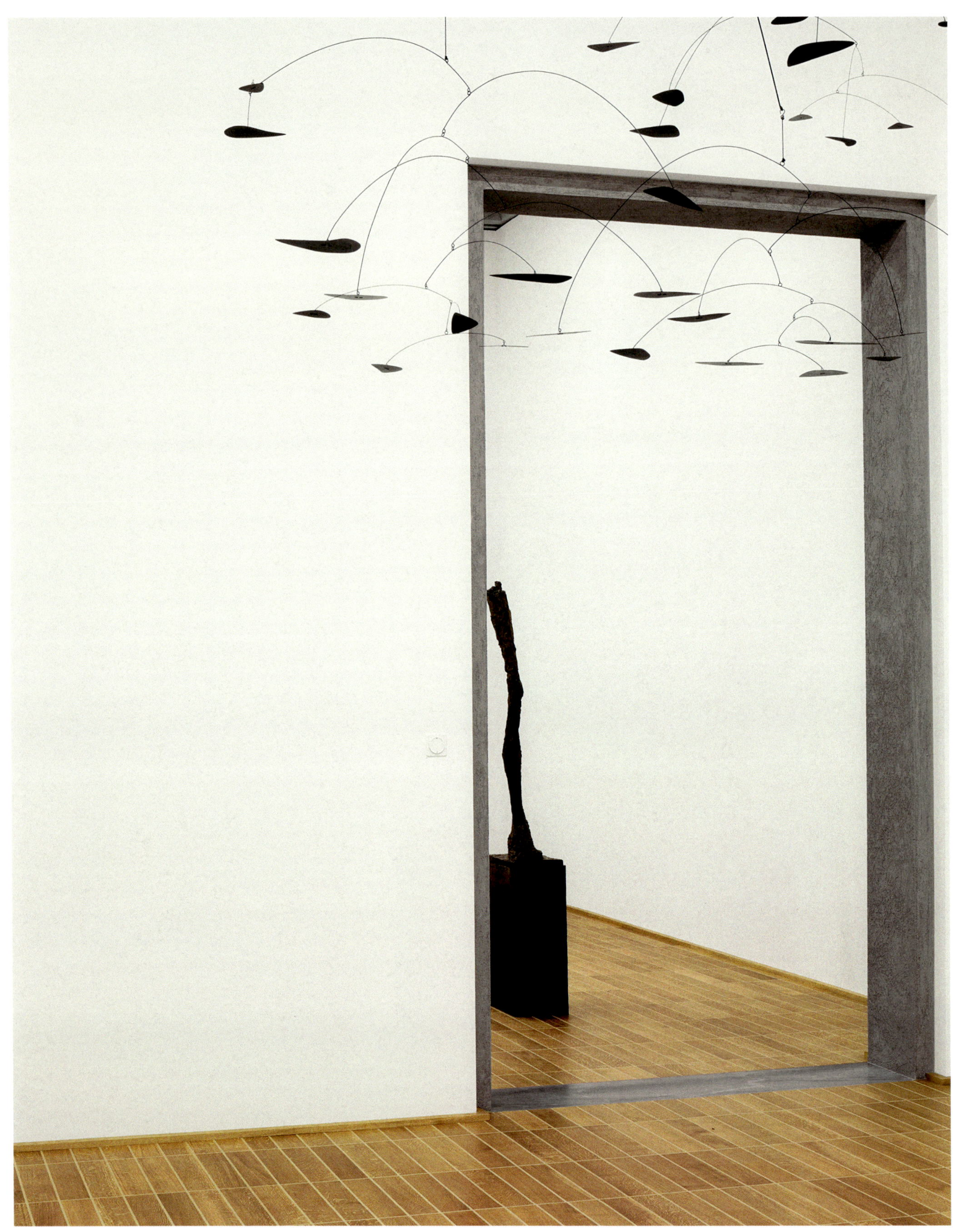

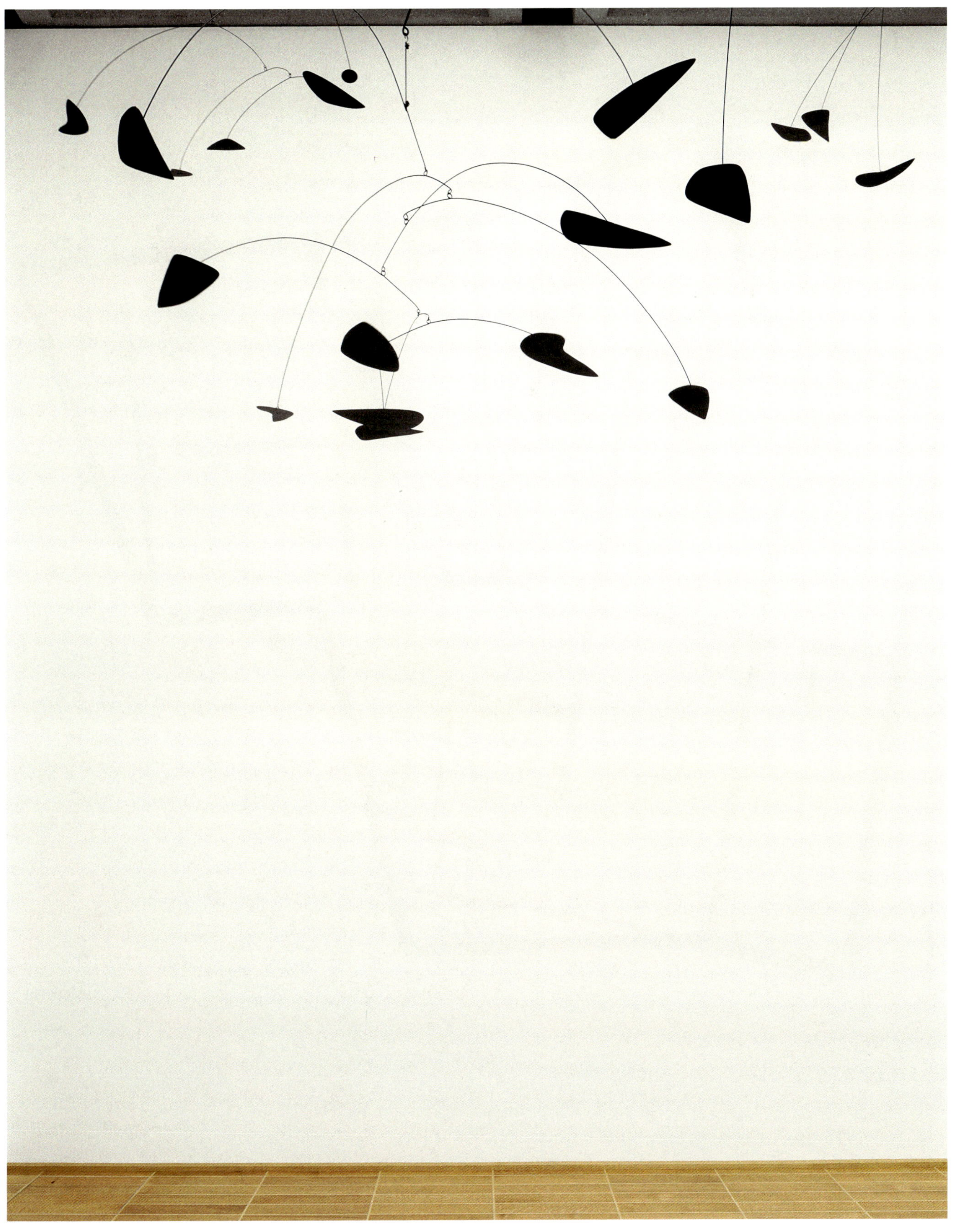

Alexander Calder, *Five Branches with 1000 Leaves*, ca. 1946 (detail), Emanuel Hoffmann Foundation, on permanent loan to the Öffentliche Kunstsammlung Basel

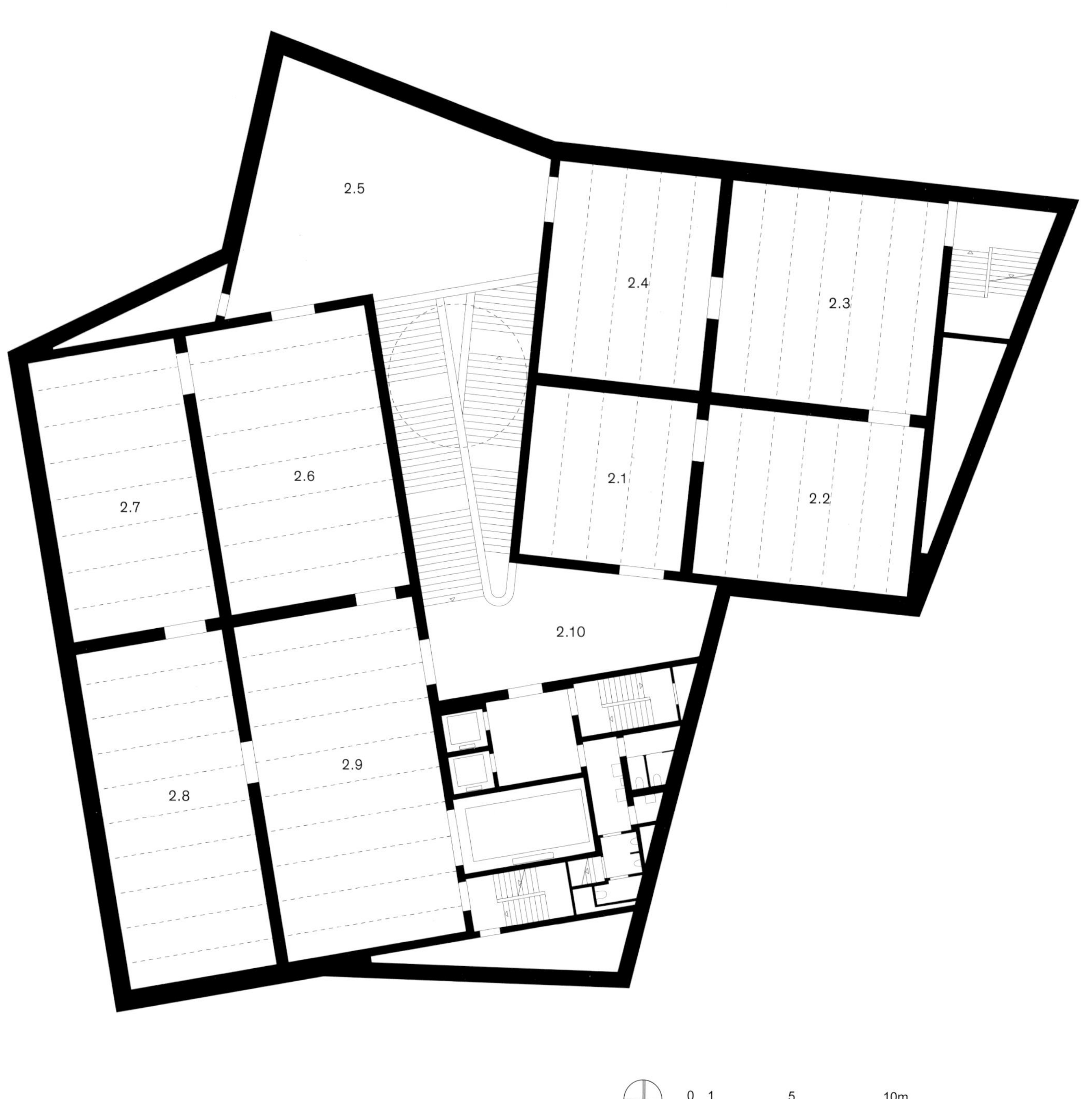

SECOND FLOOR

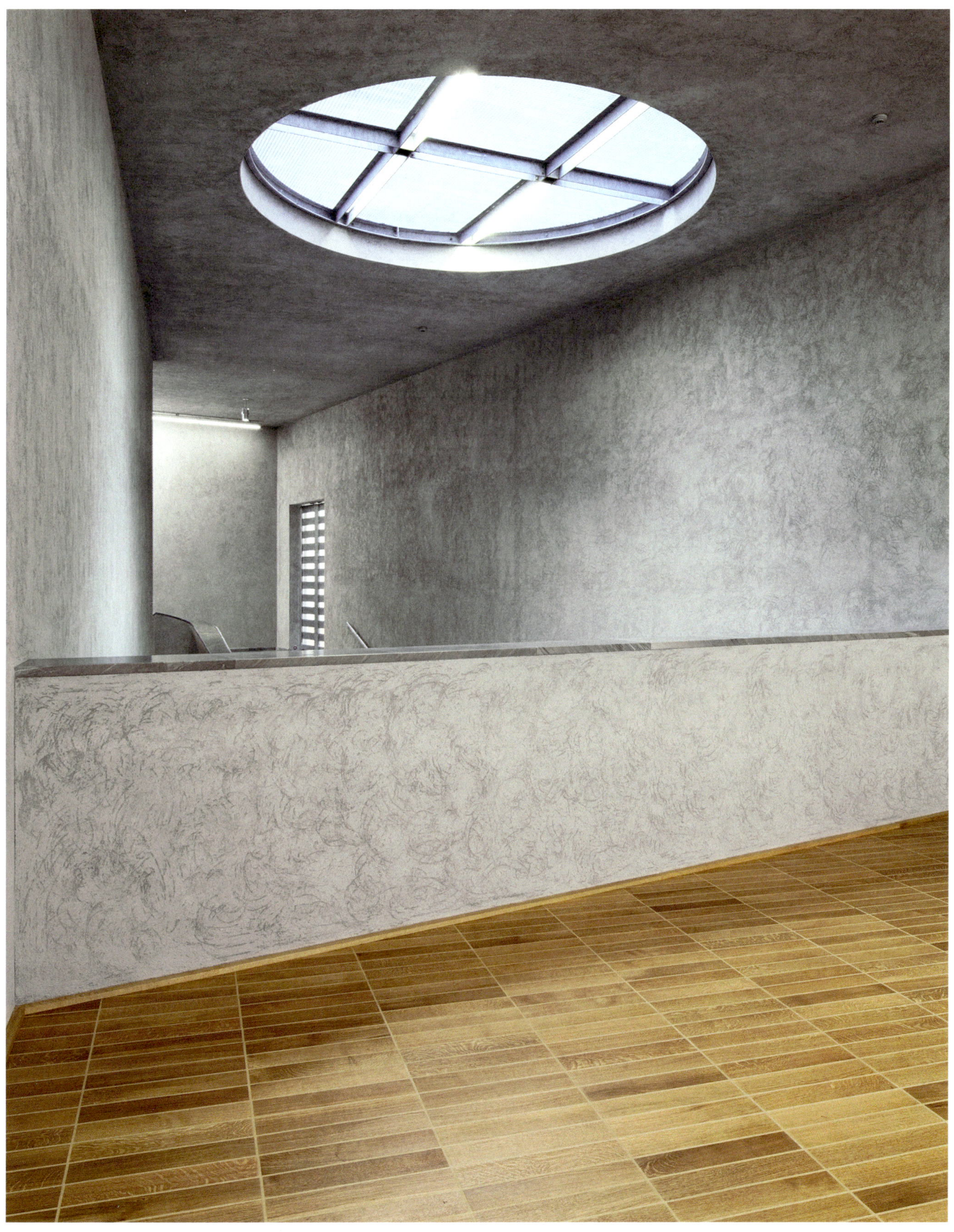

Second-floor exhibition space 2.5; view into the stairwell with skylight

A House for Art

Emanuel Christ and
Christoph Gantenbein

The extension of the Kunstmuseum Basel redefines a prominent location in the heart of the city. As a place for exhibiting and preserving art, as well as for events, the new building symbolizes both a new departure, and continuity. It is a beacon that shines not just in the city, but in the world of art and museums, too.

It is in the nature of such projects that demands on planners and architects are not just wide-ranging, but in some instances actually contradictory. In what follows, we shall explain how we have taken a stand in this project and how, in consultation with our clients, we chose to embrace some options while explicitly rejecting others as the planning process progressed. We shall endeavor to elucidate the fundamental themes that shaped our concept, the concrete ideas on which the new building rests, and our specific approach to the design process and to the work that it entailed.

ON THE OTHER SIDE OF THE STREET

First there was the site itself. Situated on the other side of the street from the existing museum, it was not the easiest point of departure for an extension; but nor was it without charms of its own. Henceforth, the new, enlarged museum was to consist of two buildings, and knowing that, we quickly intuited what the conceptual leitmotif of the new design would be. Clearly the two buildings would form a pair. New and old would be a twin presence in the urban space. What that meant for us, right from the start, was that the new building would have to reference the existing museum on several different levels at once—in other words not just functionally, but also spatially and architecturally. The new museum would be both an assertive, stand-alone building in its own right, and an extension, a new part of a larger whole that would add to and enhance what was already there, instead of vying with it. The great challenge for us, therefore, was how to lend credible form to this "not-only-but-also."

The fundamental urban figure is that of the vis-à-vis. Standing on opposite sides of the street, the two buildings enjoy a direct spatial relationship and appear as a pair in the urban space they occupy. They are the same height, meaning that the new building is "eye to eye" with the old one, just as it establishes a direct spatial relationship in other respects, too. The entrance, for example, looks across to the arcades of the old building and is clearly visible from them; the inverted corner in which the entrance is situated, moreover, can be read as an emblematic response to the similarly prominent projecting corner of the existing Kunstmuseum; the indented facade of the new building is also a gesture of welcome, an invitation. It embraces the whole intersection, turning it into its own forecourt. It is the inverted corner, furthermore, that generates the standing proportions in the facade that lend the building not just sublimity, but also a face—which is all the more important given the prominence of the location. Yet the new building is defined by more than just its location vis-à-vis the main building described here. On closer scrutiny it must also be viewed in relation to its immediate neighbors, as an integral part of both St. Alban-Vorstadt and the row of buildings along Dufourstrasse. We therefore carefully appraised how the new building would be viewed from different perspectives. Using models and drawings, we studied how high it should be, and how far back from its immediate neighbor on St. Alban-Vorstadt it would have to stand to be appreciated both as a building in its own right and as part of the row of houses on that street. The aim of all this careful sounding out of the dimensions and proportions of both the volume itself and the interstitial spaces was to model the building in such a way that it would blend in respectfully, but at the same time assertively, with its surroundings.

THE PLAN

Another challenge facing us right from the start in addition to the form of the volume was the need for an inner structure of the utmost clarity, in other words the draftsman's quest for order, proportionality, and hierarchy in the plan of the building. The outcome was its division into two distinct halves. Each floor therefore has two exhibition tracts that are connected vertically by the central, monumental staircase. Together with the foyer zones, the staircase describes a free and expressive spatial figure illuminated from above by a large round skylight. The exhibition tracts, in contrast, are intrinsically perpendicular. Their position in plan is derived from the building's larger urban context inasmuch as they run parallel to the street on either side. This allows the first-floor galleries to be side-lit, while the second floor is top-lit through the roof. Both these lighting situations were familiar to us from the main building, where they have proved their worth over the years. The overall aim was to uphold, and in a sense perpetuate, the indisputably high quality of the galleries in the main building. To ensure that every possible curatorial wish could be fulfilled, and that the new building could offer as many presentation formats as possible, we dimensioned the individual galleries in order to provide as much choice as possible with regard to both size and light. The goal was to create scope with a whole gamut of options, ranging from cabinet to hall. On average, the galleries in the new building are a good deal larger and hence more flexible than those in the old building. They also live up to classical expectations of what a museum gallery should be: namely, serene and restrained, agreeably proportioned, and made of timeless materials. These are spaces that allow art to take center stage.

COMMITTED FORM AND PHYSICAL PRESENCE

Nevertheless, the architecture of the new galleries is anything but neutral or unassuming. The rooms have a powerful, physical presence. We believe a good gallery has to commit itself in terms of both form and materials. Expressed in concrete terms, the walls have to be solid and immovable, and floor, wall, and ceiling should have a materiality that can be not just seen, but felt. Our declared goal was thus to stage these space-defining elements as clearly articulated components which, when assembled, generate a tectonics that maximizes the architectural presence of the whole.

The galleries have an industrial parquet floor made of oak strips glued directly onto the screed and grouted with wood cement. Familiar to us from workshops, commercial premises, and classrooms, this traditional flooring technique was adapted and reinterpreted to meet the specific needs of an art gallery. The strips are thus much bigger than usual, and, because they are arranged in a grid rather than with alternate joints, the grouting traces a comparatively bold pattern of lines. The wooden floor, the oak, and the floor's structural properties are not just shown; they are also staged—at least to a certain extent and in such a way that the oak parquet acquires its own distinctive architectonic presence. The supporting wall made of concrete with gray rendering is similarly explicit, as is evident from the door and window reveals. Visibly fronting these, but set back from them at the edges, is the solid, ten-centimeter-thick plasterboard wall that serves as both substrate and backdrop for the paintings. As exposed structural elements, the prefabricated, sandblasted concrete ribs that span the galleries visualize the load-bearing relationship between walls and ceiling. Not only do they lend the ceiling its own specific structure, they also give direction to the space underneath. Installed inside these ceiling elements is the artificial lighting. The standard light tubes have their own specific place as a technical, direct light source and thus become an integral, and important, part of the architecture.

THE WORK OF ART AND ITS ARCHITECTURAL COUNTERPART

This striving for tectonic presence, for an architecture that does not conceal but rather explicitly stages the structural elements out of which it is made, is predicated on the idea that the presentation of art, no matter what form it takes, will always benefit from an architecturally defined space rather than a temporary spatial situation that merely simulates architecture. In other words, the work of art needs an architectural counterpart, which in turn needs an identity of its own. Architecturally committed galleries also offer a certain friction. Both the art itself, as well as the curators have to rub up against its physical presence. This idea of rubbing up against the architecture was something we explored at length in our many discussions with Peter Fischli, who played a consultative role even at the competition stage. As both artist and curator, he has repeatedly emphasized the value and importance of powerful, robust rooms as a setting and challenge for art. Such rooms are often just as crucial to the unique and unforgettable character of the art experience as the work itself, which, after all, can be seen in temporary exhibitions in all sorts of venues all over the world. For all these reasons, we believe that works of art possess a greater intensity when shown in a committed architectural space: when an original meets an original. As orthodox and perhaps even somewhat old-fashioned as this idea might seem, in our view it is the only solution possible for a museum—especially in a world that in so many other respects is drifting further and further away from physical reality. Our intention throughout the project was to articulate an art museum as a real place for real contemplation, a place where the distillation of content translates into experiential intensity.

CONNECTING OLD AND NEW

The underground passageway that links the two buildings was especially critical, since it is here that the much-vaunted relationship between old and new takes the form of a concrete, physical space that every visitor can pass through. This operationally vital connection was to become a spatial experience that follows a dramaturgy of its own. Visitors leaving the main building via the new staircase that leads down to the passageway get a glimpse of where they are headed through the windows facing onto Dufourstrasse. The staircase is exactly modeled on the main staircase of the existing building, but in terms of its materials—the gray, veined Bardiglio marble from Carrara on the floor and rough scraped plaster in a cooler shade of gray on the walls—anticipates what lies ahead. The actual link underneath the road is not so much an underpass as a large open space leading into a generous hall that is foyer, gallery, stage, experimental space, auditorium, and function room rolled into one. The central staircase of the new building, which echoes that in the main building, starts here. The repetition of the architectural motif of the staircase in such a prominent place renders explicit what is only implied in many other places in this project: namely that the new building speaks the same, or at any rate a very similar, architectural language as the old one. The spatial and functional connection between the two buildings thus also finds expression in their shared architectural language.

This alone, however, cannot adequately explain the timeless, in places almost classical, look of the new building. For right from the start, our interest as designers extended far beyond the mere referencing and reinterpretation of the main building. Thus, while the new building does indeed speak the same language as the old, the story it tells is a new one. We understand the extension as neither a repetition nor a copy of the main building, but rather as an emphatically contemporary, forward-looking building capable of accommodating completely new forms of art. The architecture of the new building evolved out of specific technical and functional circumstances. In creating it, we were guided by our quest for a universally understandable architectural vocabulary. The forms were to be elemental, clear, and simple. Our goal was to lend the building a form of contemporary classicism.

This becomes abundantly clear in the choice of materials for the new building's foyer, where the marble flooring and galvanized steel wall cladding together form an aesthetic whole that is expressive at once of both difference and harmony. While the steel recalls industrial architecture and technical installations, the matte polished marble is more likely to conjure up images of an Italian palazzo. The one is rough and transient, the other noble and eternal. Yet it is the crossover of the two materials with their radically different connotations that generates the distinctive, unmistakable character of our building, which after all carries both within it: the time-bound technical and the eternally valid architectural.

SUSTAINABLE FORM

Perhaps the clearest expression of this theme is to be found in the facade of the new building. Its gray brick walls have a timeless, archaic, almost ruinous character. They were designed to be self-supporting and monolithic, and thanks to a sophisticated anchoring system (with elastic corners to absorb any deformations to which the building might be subject) the usual dilatation joints could be dispensed with. This in turn allowed the walls to be staged as real walls rather than cladding. What made us so determined to stage this primal architectural motif was its capacity to make manifest on the outside the very essence of what the building does on the inside, which is to create an experience that the viewer cannot help but associate with architecture's simplest and most timeless elements—walls, doors, windows, stairs, and rooms. The Kunstmuseum's new building, in other words, speaks a language that needs no translation and that will be intuitively understood for generations to come. It also speaks for itself and is thus sustainable. Viewed in this way, its elemental brick walls are also a brick-and-mortar manifesto for timeless, sustainable architecture.

SHINING BRICKS

The walls' presence is further heightened by the building's emphatic horizontality, in which the elongated bricks, just four centimeters high, are a major factor. The striking pattern of shadows cast by the alternately projecting and retracting layers of brick amplifies this impression. Such patterns are familiar to us from Italy, for example from those church facades that were never actually finished, and that even today are still waiting for the marble cladding they were promised. The horizontal grooves cut into the bricks to accommodate the anchors are still clearly visible—only the project never advanced that far.

The Kunstmuseum's new building with its brick facade might also be said to carry within it a certain latency, an unfinished aspect, or at any rate the quality of understatement. The extension is clearly holding back, allowing the old building to take precedence. Our choice of brick as the "poor" relation of the limestone slabs of the main building was deliberate. The idea was to show that both buildings were "handcrafted," that is to say, built brick by brick, the only difference being in the materials. The distinction also visualizes the clear hierarchy that exists between them. Like the facade of the main building, that of the new building follows the standard tripartite order of Classical architecture. This order is visualized on the one hand through the brickwork's different shades of gray, and on the other through a frieze executed as a fine relief. The frieze, in its archetypal form, has always been part of the traditional architectural canon, but in the form it takes here represents something quite new: sunk into the grooves of the frieze blocks are strips of LEDs that, by illuminating the hollows between the bricks, shed an indirect light into the surrounding urban space. The result is a visually stimulating effect as the archaic-looking masonry begins to shine, or at least to glow. Thus a wall that might otherwise look ordinary is—quite literally—electrified. We imagine this subtle form of lighting, which appears to emanate from within the brick walls themselves, to be a very modern form of radiance. The abstract patterns that echo the horizontality of the wall—not just in form, but also in light and shade and in words and images, and in so doing speak of what is inside the museum—promise to turn the outer shell of the new building into something animate, engaged in an ongoing dialogue with the viewer. The new building will indeed express—literally "radiate"—the idea that guided us right from the start: that the new building should be a house for art, at once both protective and open.

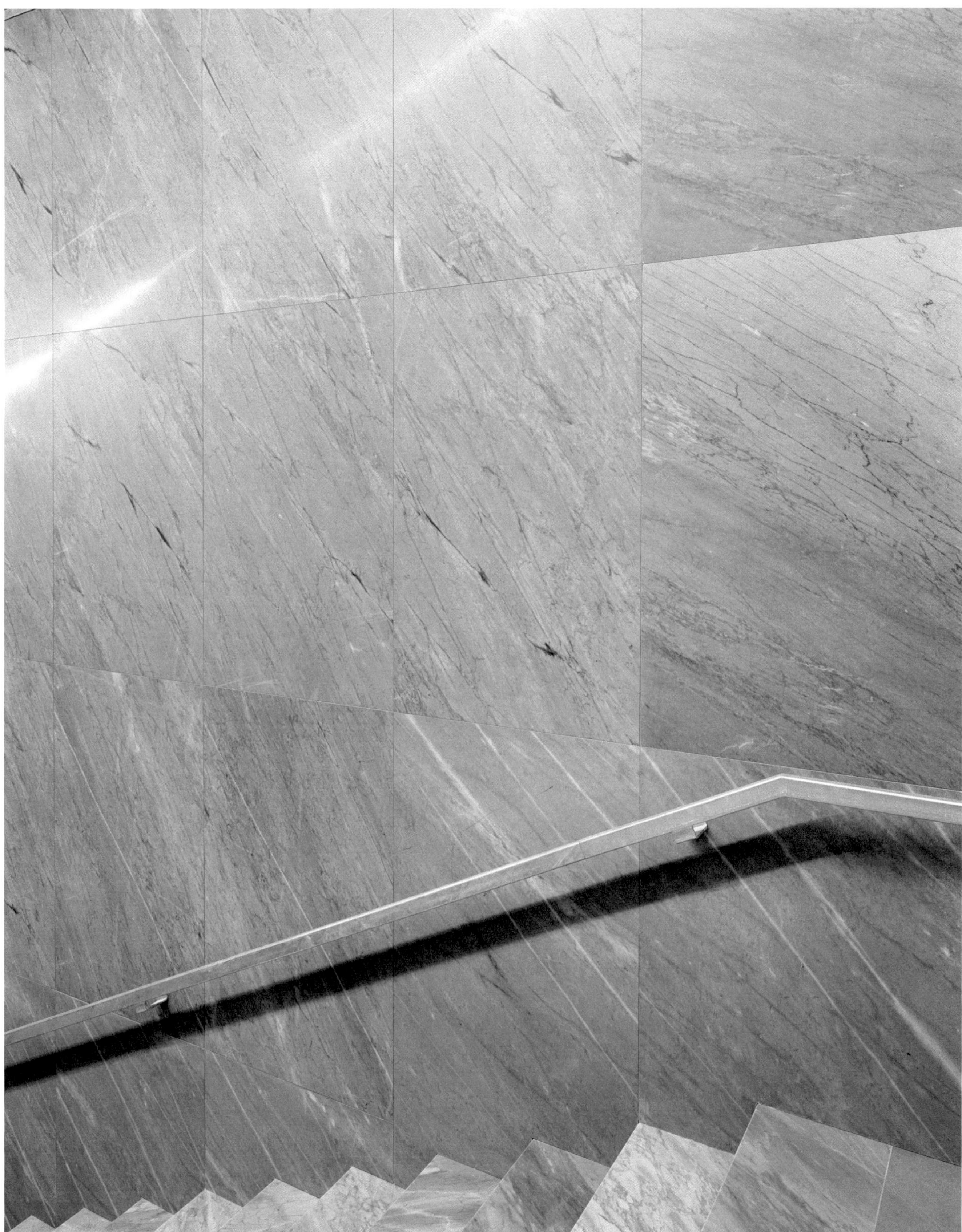

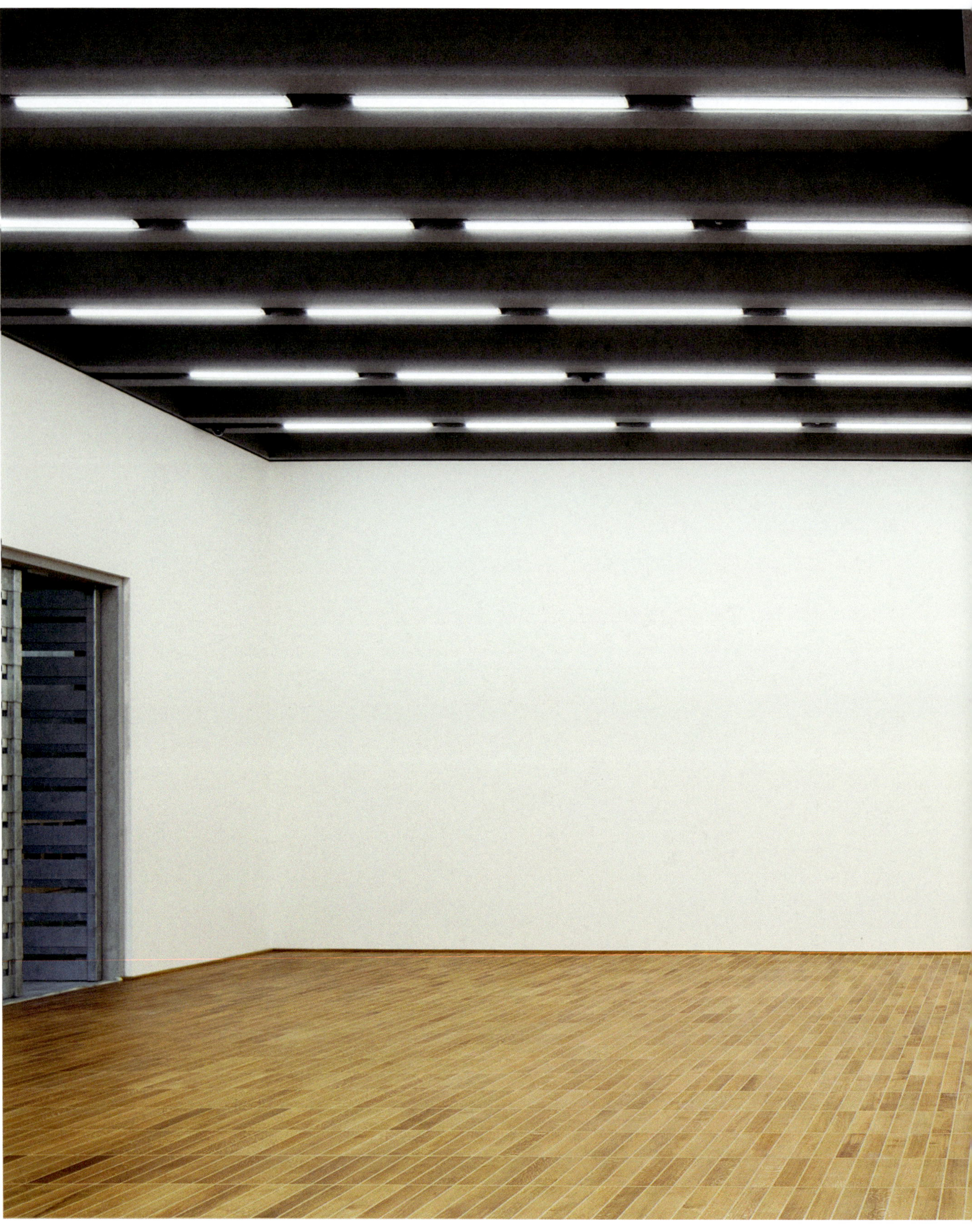

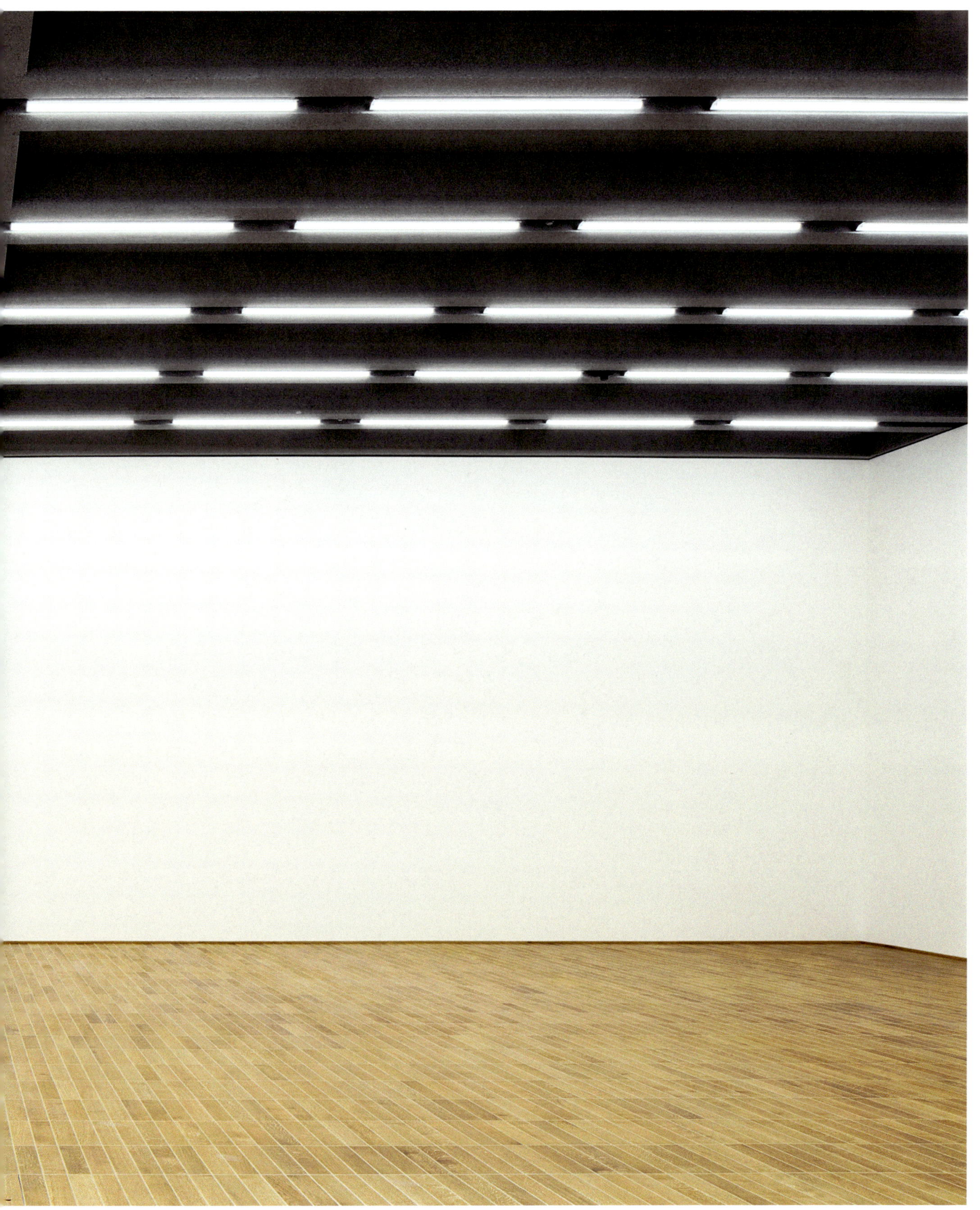

Column-free exhibition space on the ground floor

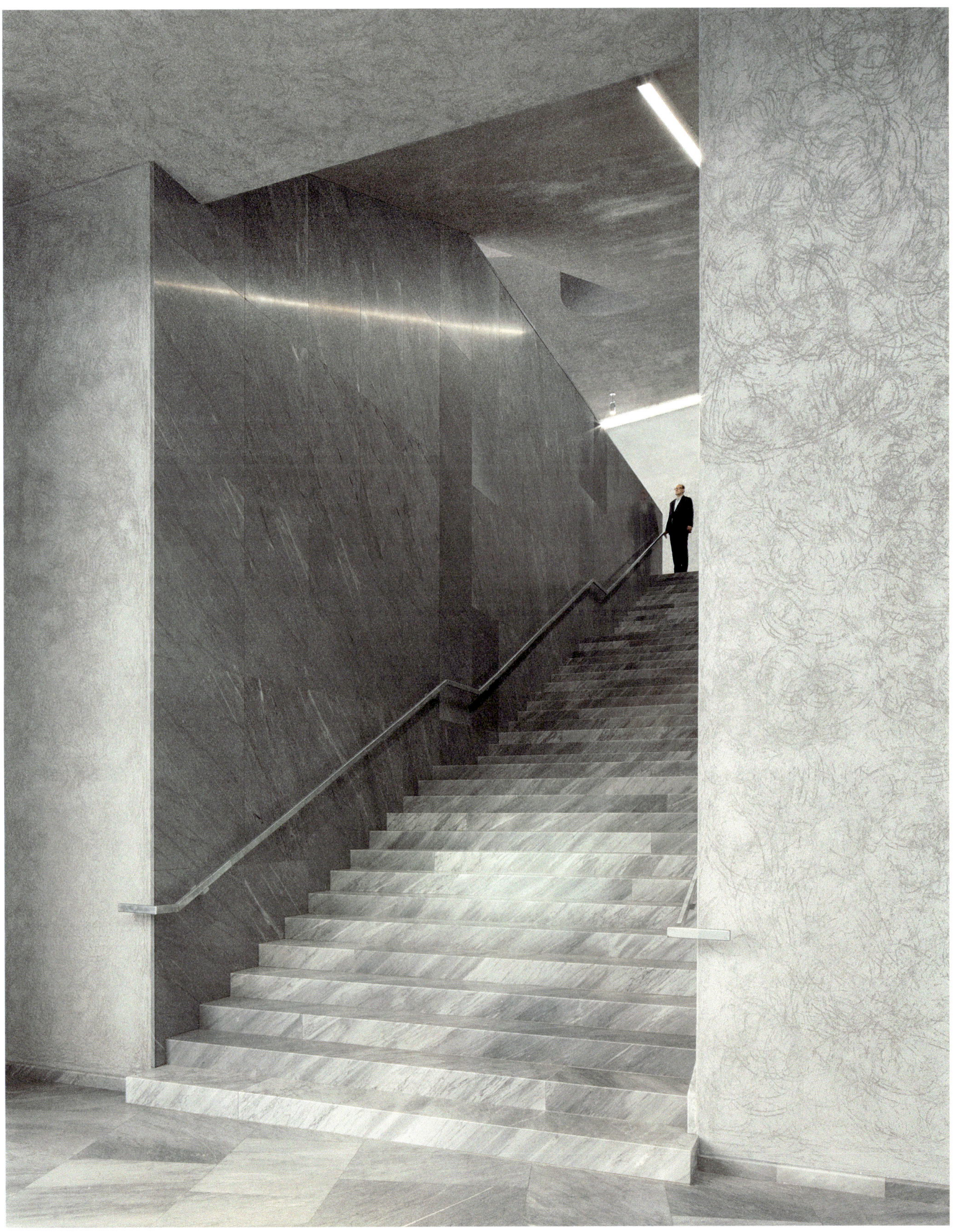

Stairs to first lower level

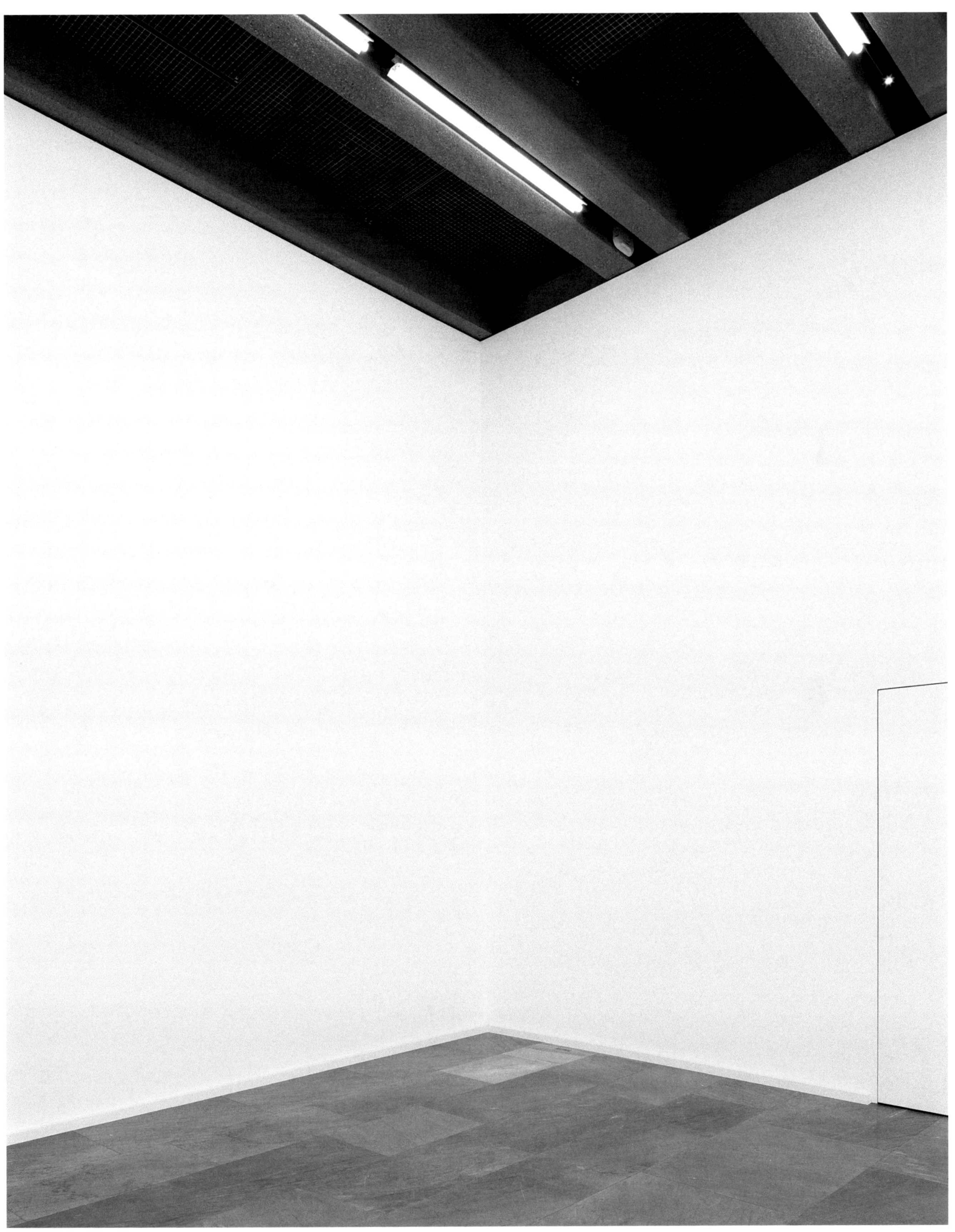

Lower-level foyer

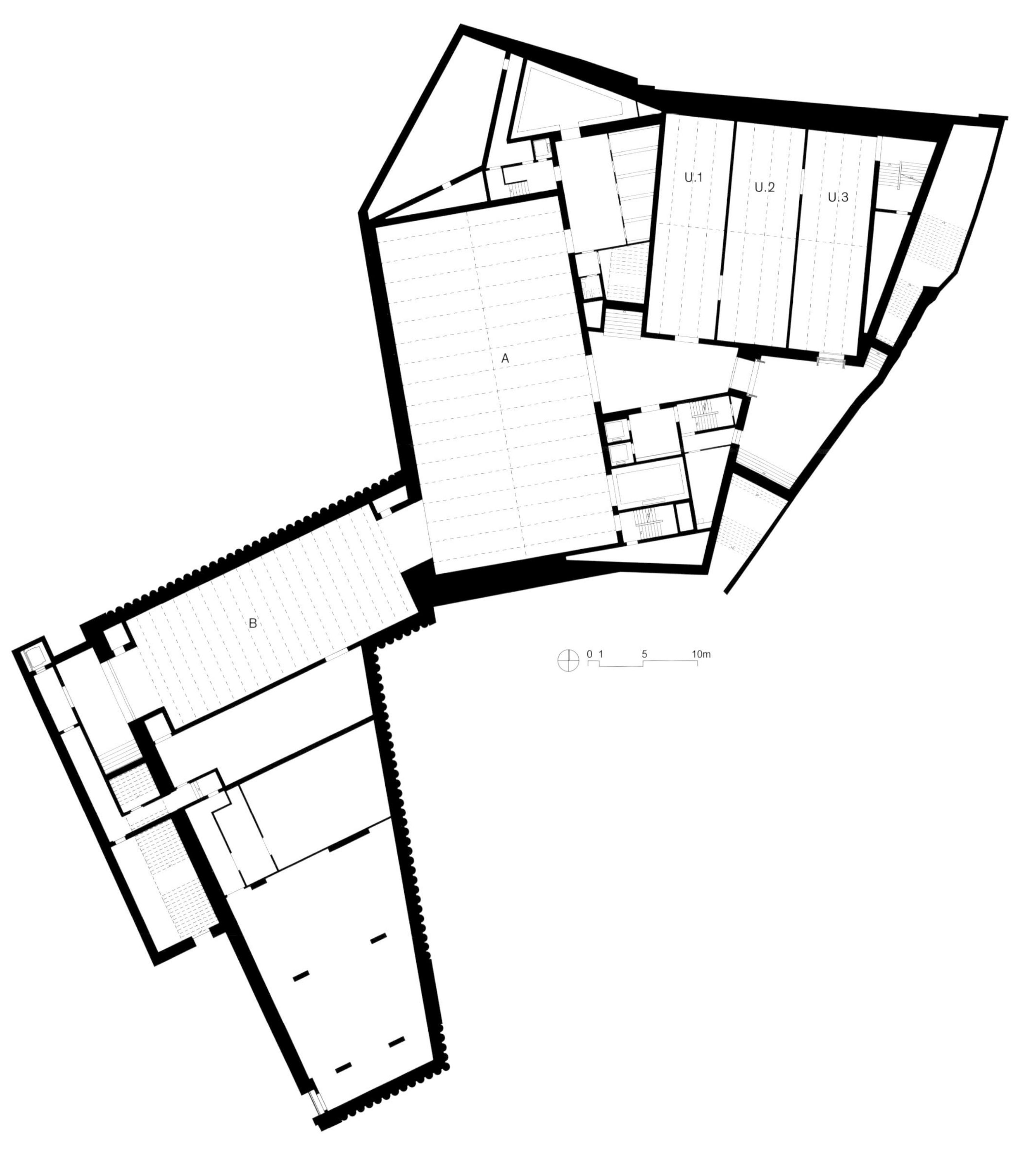

FIRST LOWER LEVEL
A Foyer / B Passageway / U.1–U.3 Exhibition spaces

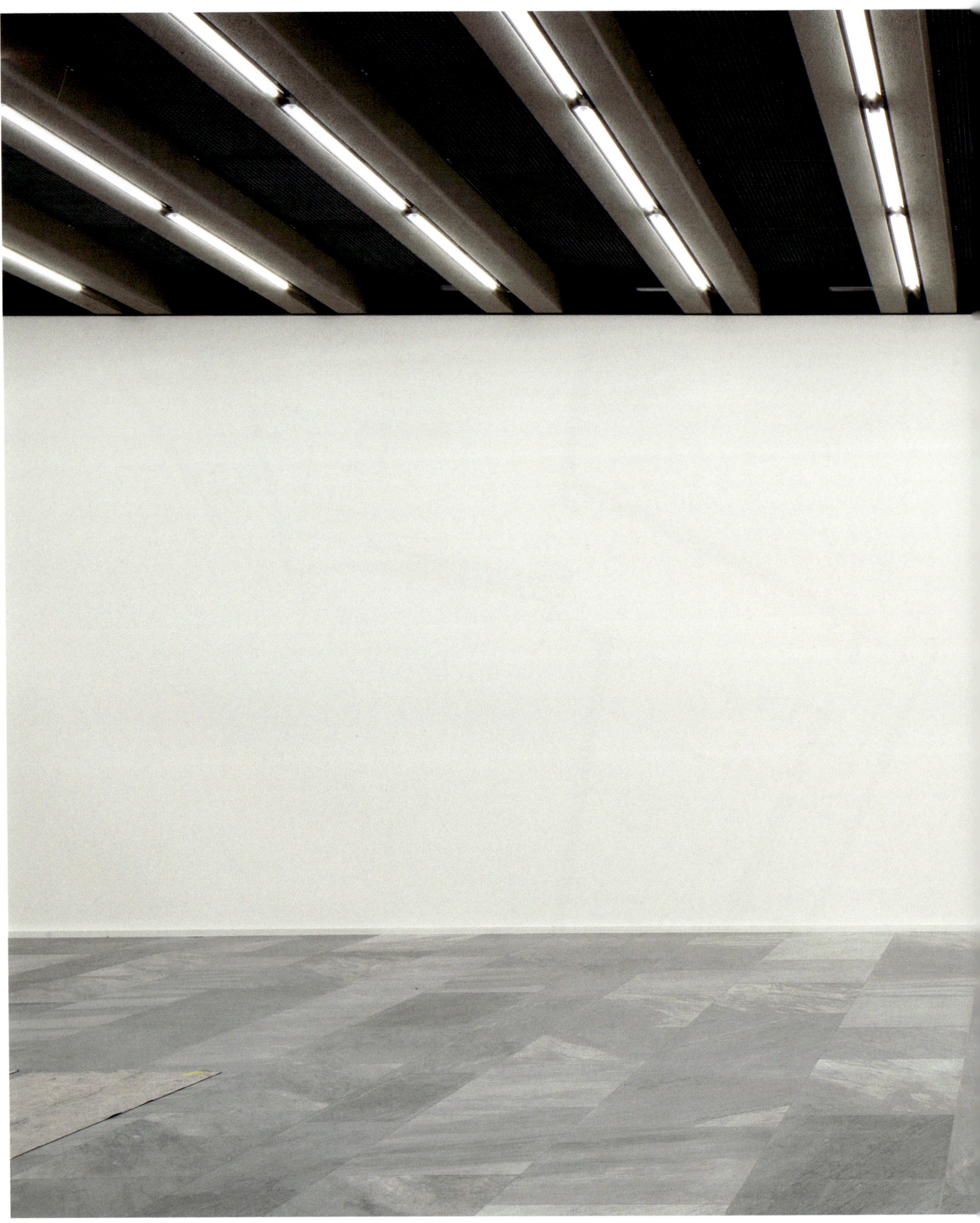

First lower-level foyer with marble floor, plasterboard walls, and concrete ceiling elements with linear LED lighting

A Building Is Concerned with the Present On the Kunstmuseum Basel's New Building by Christ & Gantenbein

Mechtild Widrich

The words of Adolf Loos, to whom I owe the title of this essay, are certainly memorable, but they are only half of the equation. Loos defined the difference between art and architecture with customary succinctness: "The work of art ... thinks of the future," he wrote. "A building is concerned with the present." [1] Even if the dichotomy is not one we would necessarily still subscribe to, the distinction drawn is an astonishingly apposite description of the challenge posed by the extension of the Kunstmuseum Basel. The task of creating an architectural setting for works of modern and contemporary art that would not only do justice to a forward-looking present (and past), but would at the same time incorporate the presence of an existing museum was surely a daunting one. What would the ideal case be? Presumably a building that addressed the factors that drive art not just institutionally, but architecturally, too. To fulfill this ideal, a museum of modern and contemporary art would have to engage with two crucial—and at first sight contradictory—impulses of twentieth- and twenty-first-century art: autonomy and context. Upholding art's autonomy from political or social strictures in architectural terms means delivering enough neutral physical space for the objects themselves, and enough mental space for visitors to contemplate them. Historically, the white cube with its whitewashed, windowless walls was thought to be the perfect answer—and at the same time the ultimate critique of the neoclassical museum of the nineteenth century, whose profusion of ornament functioned like a kind of bourgeois straitjacket for art objects both sacred and secular. Yet even as early as the late nineteen-sixties, the white cube itself came to seem suspect. Not only did its spatial neutrality and the absolute autonomy of the exhibits turn a visit to the art gallery into a suffocatingly devotional experience, or so it was argued, but its exclusion of the outside world accorded the art a purity such as might be understood only by a noiseless, and perhaps bodiless, visitor—an eye without a body, as it were—and, by cutting the objects off from life, invested them with an immutability that they did not possess.[2] So what might be the alternative? In a recent article called "After the White Cube," the critic Hal Foster analyzed the recent shift away from the notion of exhibition architecture as a seemingly neutral interior space.[3] The alternative model, says Foster, is the "museum as icon"—a readily digestible demonstration of architecture as spectacle provided primarily to boost tourism and generate a media buzz, as did the monumentally sculptural Guggenheim Bilbao by Frank O. Gehry, for example. The contemplation of the works of art exhibited in such a place inevitably becomes a secondary matter. Related to this is a third type, namely the museum as event space, of which Renzo Piano's new Whitney Museum of American Art in New York is a case in point. The buildings in this category are open and transparent, typically with a vast expanse of glass that forces those on the inside to look out. In the eyes of art historian Sarah K. Rich, they are manifestations of the "cultural appetite for art that is in the world and of it," invested with what—with just a hint of irony—she calls a "sunny

1 Adolf Loos, "Architektur" (1910), in idem, *Trotzdem. 1900–1930*, Innsbruck 1931, pp. 90–104, here p. 101. For an English version of this text, see http://www.mom.arq.ufmg.br/mom/arq_interface/2a_aula/loos_architecture.pdf (last accessed February 2016).

2 The best known texts from this period are those by Brian O'Doherty, whose series of essays called "Inside the White Cube" was published by *Artforum* in 1976.

3 Hal Foster, "After the White Cube," *London Review of Books*, 37, 6, March 19, 2015, pp. 25–26, http://www.lrb.co.uk/v37/n06/hal-foster/after-the-white-cube (last accessed December 2015).

design."[4] The dramatic gesture that Rich identifies in Piano's expansive architecture is also an urbanist bid for power in New York's Meatpacking District. If the museum fits in at all, then it is only in the fast-paced dynamic of urban development.

I. That I chose to open a text about the Kunstmuseum Basel's new building by Christ & Gantenbein with a current typology of the museum has to do with more than just my profession as a historian. The two architects are themselves well versed in history. In his essay "About Architecture for Art," for example, Christoph Gantenbein describes a spectrum ranging from the museum as bourgeois institution, a place to visit on Sunday afternoons (dragging the children along, of course) to the multipurpose cultural centers of the nineteen-seventies to today's international temples of highbrow consumerism.[5] Of special importance to our understanding of the new extension is the meaning of the whole concept of typology in the works of Christ & Gantenbein, by which I mean the form prevailing for a specific function in a specific temporal and geographical context. "Typology" is indeed a fundamental premise for both architects, and not just for their buildings, but also for architecture per se, which explains their choice of the term as the title of their two-volume compendium published in 2012 and 2015.[6] The lavishly illustrated studies in that work subject the typologies of buildings in cities as diverse as Buenos Aires, Hong Kong, Rome, Athens, Paris, and Delhi to critical, in-depth analysis. The focus is on the overall form, footprint, and volumes of the buildings, and on their flexibility and versatility. According to Christ & Gantenbein, types should always be conceived as unstable constructs, since they develop on the basis of factors outside the realm of architecture (including aesthetic factors) and are therefore liable to come under pressure as soon as the context changes. This rational approach has less to do with the history of a radical break with tradition (as does Modernism, for example) or with referencing some randomly selected historical position (as does Postmodernism) than with sounding out the possibilities of a given locale. It is to the dimension of time that we have to look in order to find a happy medium between Modernism's avant-gardism and Postmodernism's historicist paraphrasing and recapitulation—a happy medium whose emphasis is on a situation of presence that manifests itself spatially and is open both to the past and to what is yet to come. "Modernist architects," wrote Gantenbein in 2012, "were convinced that the only way to improve a situation was to apply a tabula rasa strategy or at least to implement a project that anticipated a radical replacement of an existing reality. In contrast, we develop our designs directly out of a given situation with the ambition to interact with it, to reinterpret it, or to carefully change it."[7]

4 Sarah K. Rich, "Brought to Light. The New Whitney Museum of American Art," *Artforum* 54, September 2015, pp. 350–353, here p. 351.

5 Christoph Gantenbein, "Über Architektur für die Kunst" (interview recorded on December 16, 2012), in Nele Dechmann and Nicola Ruffo (eds.), *Architektur im Würgegriff der Kunst*, Zurich 2013, pp. 93–101.

6 Emanuel Christ, Christoph Gantenbein, et al. (eds.), *Typology. Hong Kong, Rome, New York, Buenos Aires*, Zurich 2012; idem, *Typology. Paris, Delhi, São Paulo, Athens*, Zurich 2015. There is a point of connection with Loos here. In "Architektur" (Loos 1931, see note 1), p. 103, Loos writes: "To secret vice the law courts must seem to make the threatening gesture. A bank must say, 'Here your money is safe in the hands of honest people.'" The typological method, however, is even more discerningly defined in the first sentence of the next paragraph: "An architect can only achieve this by going back to those buildings of the past which aroused those moods in people."

7 Christoph Gantenbein, quoted from "Two Buildings. Emanuel Christ and Christoph Gantenbein in Conversation with Victoria Easton," in Markus Breitschmid and Victoria Easton, *Christ & Gantenbein. Around the Corner*, Ostfildern 2012, pp. 49–79, here p. 55.

II. Typology for Christ & Gantenbein is first and foremost the possibility of taking the concrete context of a given project as the point of departure for its design. An extension, for example, is by definition part of the existing urban fabric. Christ & Gantenbein therefore see their projects as embodying "research into the relationship between the architectural object and the city."[8] More to the point, it means that every architectural design is simultaneously always also an urban design ... It follows that form is crucial: "We are convinced that all these substantive and spatial relationships must be reflected in the building. Architectural form is a matter of putting things in relationship with the city."[9]

To understand this, we have only to look at the form and volume of the Kunstmuseum Basel's new building, in other words at those parameters that are instantly visible in the urban space. The volume as a whole with its strategically positioned windows seems self-contained and firmly anchored, although its heavy, monolithic quality is somewhat attenuated by the brick facade with its fine gradations of gray. The brick, which by nature is but a "humble material," according to the architects, takes up the color of the bands of a darker hue that break up the expanse of plain cut stone that forms the facade of the main building. If the frieze on that building was itself an elegant abstraction of its classical forebears, its darker tonal values, abstracted again as a kind of plinth, are scaled so as to lend the extension an upward dynamic.[10] Then, immediately above the windows, there really is a frieze, a 3.08-m-high band of darker brick that provides a formal link with the main building. Nor is that all. The white LEDs sunk into the mortar not only allow the building to speak, but also offer enormous artistic scope, including for visualizations. Those who cringe at the idea of the facade as spectacle can rest assured that the frieze is so discreet that it scarcely stands out at all. And while it invites experimentation going beyond that permitted by a billboard or marquee, it is certainly not dominant.[11] The invitation to the city also informs the plastic configuration of the concave angle opening onto the corner of St. Alban-Graben and Dufourstrasse, which is where the entrance is located. While this corner location, unlike the arcades of the main building, makes the extension part of a public square, it does not actually interlock with street space.[12] Without pomp, without show, the new building "opens its arms" to the city, inviting its residents to let it affect them. Such an invitation must be actively apprehended, however, since this is not a transparent structure whose inner workings are there for all to see; nor is it a machine—like the Centre Pompidou in Paris—whose structure spills over into urban space. The facade is too hermetic for that; the building itself too monumentally self-contained.

8 Emanuel Christ and Christoph Gantenbein, "Typology Transfer—Towards an Urban Architecture" (inaugural lecture at the ETH Zürich, November 30, 2011), in Christ/Gantenbein 2012 (see note 6), pp. 3–15, here p. 4.

9 Ibid., pp. 4–6.

10 In their inaugural lecture at the ETH, the architects spoke of the brick facade as an "ärmlichen Material" with connotations of ruins. I would prefer to talk of age. Cf. Christ/Gantenbein 2012 (see note 6), p. 6. For more on the main building, cf. Rudolf Christ and Otto Fischer, *Kunstmuseum Basel*, Basel 1937, and the Verein der Freunde des Kunstmuseums and the Museums für Gegenwartskunst Basel (eds.), *Kunstmuseum Basel. Die Architektur*, Basel 2003.

11 Here we might almost imagine an allusion to the "Decorated Shed"—that neutral, modular building with advertising ("I am a Monument"), that Robert Venturi and Denise Scott Brown cast in opposition to the architecturally planned monument ("Duck"). The "Decorated Shed" is on a par with the white cube.

12 Rudolf Christ, "Der Bau," in Christ/Fischer 1937 (see note 10), p. 9.

The decision to locate the connection between the museum and its extension underground, rather than having a conspicuous bridge or even robbing Dufourstrasse, as the thoroughfare in-between, of its airspace by building right over it, is a measure of the architects' appreciation of the value of a mature urban environment. The idea was not to bind the buildings together to the exclusion of the city of which they are a part, but to emphasize the new building's desired status as a link in the chain connecting the main building and the Kunstmuseum Basel | Gegenwart—the Museum of Contemporary Art. The strategy of staging the parity between the two via the symmetry of obtuse angles "turned on their heads," and instantly eye-catching "acute formations" may seem rather formalist at first.[13] A glance at history and at the urban situation of the main building by Paul Bonatz and Rudolf Christ, built between 1931 and 1936, and at how it relates to the present may prove enlightening here, just as it may help explain the architects' formal decisions in relation to Basel as a city of art. The year 1661, when the city of Basel and the university acted in concert to avert the impending loss of the Amerbach-Kabinett, and to ensure that its treasures, including several works by Hans Holbein the Younger, could henceforth be enjoyed and appreciated by the public at large, can with good reason be regarded as the date of birth of the public art collection. The private became communal and the communal became public, which is a very different backstory from that of countless other European museums of the eighteenth and nineteenth centuries, most of which grew out of great aristocratic collections, as the extensive research done in this field tells us. If the history of the collection of the Kunstmuseum Basel is read from the premises it has occupied, the story they tell is one of a shortage of space, several relocations, and finally, in the late-1920s, the decision to build a dedicated new museum on a prominent, downtown site. The building of the extension was likewise motivated by lack of space—space not just for major exhibitions,[14] but also for "temporary presentations" of a steadily expanding collection.[15]

Christ & Gantenbein counter the structural instability inherent both in the commitment to continue acquiring art and in the predictable unpredictability of the demands that special exhibitions might yet make of the architecture with what they call an "engaged" spatial concept that manifests itself in an emphasis on tectonics, in other words on material presence and design.[16] This engagement, which Christ & Gantenbein achieve both physically and sociologically, is in part a reaction to the practice of staging exhibitions with the aid of flexible room dividers, which brings its own set of problems with it. But it can also be attributed to the specifics of Basel's identity as the host city of one of the world's largest art fairs, Art Basel. There, unlike in museums, first-rate art is displayed on movable partitions in close proximity to hundreds of other works. The architecture,

13 Markus Breitschmid has argued for the existence of "the tendency toward acute formations," in his essay "Built Sublimation The Architecture of Christ & Gantenbein," in Breitschmid/Easton 2012 (see note 7), pp. 165–230, here p. 167.

14 Bernhard Mendes Bürgi, "Ausgangslage und Ziel," in Hochbau und Planungsamt des Kantons Basel Stadt (ed.), *Kunstmuseum Basel. Erweiterungsbau "Burghof." Anonymer Projektwettbewerb im selektiven Verfahren*, Final Report, December 2009, p. 5.

15 Bernhard Mendes Bürgi, "Aufgabe," ibid., pp. 13–23, here p. 13. The demands made of a *Kunstmuseum*, in other words, have to be combined with those of a *Kunsthalle* for special exhibitions only.

16 Interview with Emanuel Christ, Basel, May 2015.

moreover, is flexible enough to be able to respond instantly to the exhibitors' purchasing power. In reality, the ostensibly neutral whitewashed walls could scarcely be more highly charged; it is as if the whole constellation were crying out for a "tectonically present" architecture.[17] That here, too, "presence" means not some fleeting event, but rather the expansive presence of a spatial necessity that takes account of what comes before and after, behind and beside, is legible in the architecture itself. The interior spaces can be felt, the walls are fixed, and the partitioning is unambiguous. The rooms neither deny their function as exhibition spaces, nor are they either capricious or dominant. Details such as the relatively low window ledges that alert us to the transition from inside to out—that force us to make up our minds and direct our gaze either inward or outward—are likewise a manifestation of this same principle of engagement.

III. Extensions bring their own special temporality with them. After all, whether they reference it, offer a formal continuation of it, or even reject it, their point of reference is the museum that is already there and the history of that building. So far, I have discussed the facade's formal referencing of the main building as a form of "communication" that is also a source of productive tension—arising from the difficulty of reconciling the notion of communication with the main building's alleged autonomy. Looking at the typology of the extensions which since the 1970s have been built onto art galleries and museums of modern art erected within the past hundred years or so, one is struck by their heterogeneity—a heterogeneity so great that it is hard to make out any direction at all. The grounds most often cited for such additions, as one would expect, are the need to accommodate acquisitions and gifts, and the fact that contemporary artists since the 1950s have been producing ever larger works, although changed expectations with regard to hanging and the museum experience per se are also factors. The best known of those extensions that physically encroach on an existing museum come across as somewhat theatrical challenges to the Humanist claims of an earlier era. Daniel Libeskind's explosion of crystalline shapes emanating from the Royal Ontario Museum in Toronto (2007) is a good example of this. It involves visitors in a "permanent drama" that is deliberately at odds with the excessively static museum concept of the nineteenth century.[18] Formal qualities like open (transparent) and closed, serenity and dynamism, here become metaphors of the extremes of what visitors actually experience—metaphors whose application in reality, no matter how indisputably impressive, is bound to remain controversial. In the case of the Sainsbury Wing of London's National Gallery of 1991 designed by Robert Venturi and Denise Scott Brown, a shining example of the formal reference, the paraphrase is so close that it becomes ironic, which in its turn creates distance and perhaps betrays a fundamental ambivalence on the part of the architects vis-à-vis the old building, and museums generally. Christ & Gantenbein are predisposed neither to pathos-laden gestures nor to critical introspection. And even if their extension of the Swiss National Museum in Zurich relies on angular elevations and emphatically round windows, the

17 Christoph Gantenbein, "In this sense, what we have developed for the Kunstmuseum is an almost expressive, tectonic architecture, a work of great presence that lends materiality to space." Gantenbein 2013 (see note 5), p. 96.
18 Marcus Fairs, "Daniel Libeskind at Royal Ontario Museum," in *Dezeen Magazine*, May 14, 2007, http://www.dezeen.com/2007/05/14/daniel-libeskind-at-royal-ontario-musem/ (last accessed December 2015).

ensemble is neither Modernist rebuttal nor Postmodernist parody, but rather a thoughtful analysis of a historicist original with carefully chosen innovations, such as the aforementioned round windows.

Even more instructive is the encounter with the project that in 2013 won the architects the competition for an extension of the Wallraf-Richartz-Museum & Fondation Corboud in Cologne, whose point of reference was a product of the recent past: a building by Oswald Mathias Ungers that opened in 2001. Here, too, Christ & Gantenbein chose to work in brick—in this case red brick, which can be interpreted as more than just a nod to the existing buildings nearby, Cologne's Roman origins, and northern Europe's long tradition of using red brick as a building material. The form is a cube framed at both top and bottom and here, too, it is the frieze that plays the key role, becoming a plinth whose faux timber framing opens up the monolithic volume, and in doing so communicates with the surrounding urban space. On closer inspection, the posts and beams turn out to be a line of writing: WALLRAF RICHARTZ CORBOUD—the names of the founders Ferdinand Franz Wallraf and Johann Heinrich Richartz, and of Gérard J. Corboud, carry the new extension. The ambiguity of the frieze, which is neither unequivocally a line of writing nor abstract decoration, translates both the tradition of timber framing and the art of dedication into a contemporary architectural idiom.

The monumental quality in the works of Christ & Gantenbein, I would therefore argue, resides also—perhaps even primarily—in their ability to integrate temporal components in a spatial configuration. In Basel, as in Cologne, the friezes are a factor that is both time-defining and monumentalizing, if only because we ourselves have to move and need time to read them—and hence to appreciate them—in their entirety. The buildings are thus monuments in the true sense of the word, inasmuch as they distill historicity for the present, enabling time to become form. That this is not done narratively, but through a subtle play of forms is what makes this approach so special. The best evidence of this in Basel are the interior details. The rough scraped plaster on the walls of the entrance area is an especially attractive feature, scraped plasterwork being a centuries-old technique in both Italy and Germany, which in the twentieth century enjoyed a revival after Walter Gropius used it for the Bauhaus building in Dessau (1925/26); hence the rough scraped plaster to underscore the pragmatic Modernism of the main building, too.[19] The rendering generally is an important detail, not least in relation to the positioning of architecture and art object. While on the one hand it is restrained, on the other it serves to relieve the monotony and to debunk the whitewashed walls' claim to "absence" or "neutrality"—even if the walls in the galleries themselves are indeed neutral white.

The floors made of marble or industrial parquet have a similar function, providing just enough structure to make the solidity of the architecture a palpable experience, while articulating it visually at the same time. The parquet with wood cement grouting recalls the auditorium of the main building as well as other examples in buildings belonging to the University of Basel. While the pattern is essentially the same, it was enlarged and adapted to the contemporary

19 The walls of the main building were originally covered with textiles and even faux fur. See Christ/Fischer 1937 (see note 10).

preference for calmer, less busy forms than those of the first half of the twentieth century. Especially striking in the exhibition spaces are the ceilings, which derive a certain solidity from their raw concrete ribs only to be instantly relieved of it by the linear LED lighting installed inside them. The necessary infrastructure, in this case light, serves as a counterweight to the massiveness of the concrete, casting doubt on its materiality and answering its bulk with illuminated negative space, infusing it with a lightness it would otherwise lack. The staircase is another good example, for as monolithic as it is—an effect underscored by the use of marble—the horseshoe shape with first-floor landing makes it so much an integral part of the architecture that it is perceived as open and dynamic and not at all as overbearing and ostentatious.

The references to the main building (including the plasterwork, the floors, the dimensioning of the staircase) are experienced by visitors in the here and now, yet rely on their ability to recall the other building in order to connect the two. This time shift, this resurfacing of details that can be experienced either before or after in the other building, exposes the historicity of architecture—and not just of architecture. For ultimately, what Christ & Gantenbein reveal to us is that the experience of the present, be it of art or architecture, always reaches back into the past and forward into the future, which is why the idea of a museum is not, in fact, at odds with forward-looking contemporary art after all. For ultimately, Christ & Gantenbein's typology is a typology of temporality, an architecture of presence that carries both memory and expectation within it, and that can unfold only through physical and intellectual interaction with the visitor who is actually there.

IV. The most astonishing design by Adolf Loos is surely his "great Greek-style column" in black granite of 1922 that was to have housed the *Chicago Tribune*. Looking yet again at this strangely archaic, corporate tombstone that could scarcely stay standing in the present, one is bound to question the degree to which typology alone can bring forth something new from something old. In Basel, Christ & Gantenbein have engaged us in a discourse of past and future, autonomy and context, art and city that is much more subtle; and the result is a building that even in the future will think of the present.

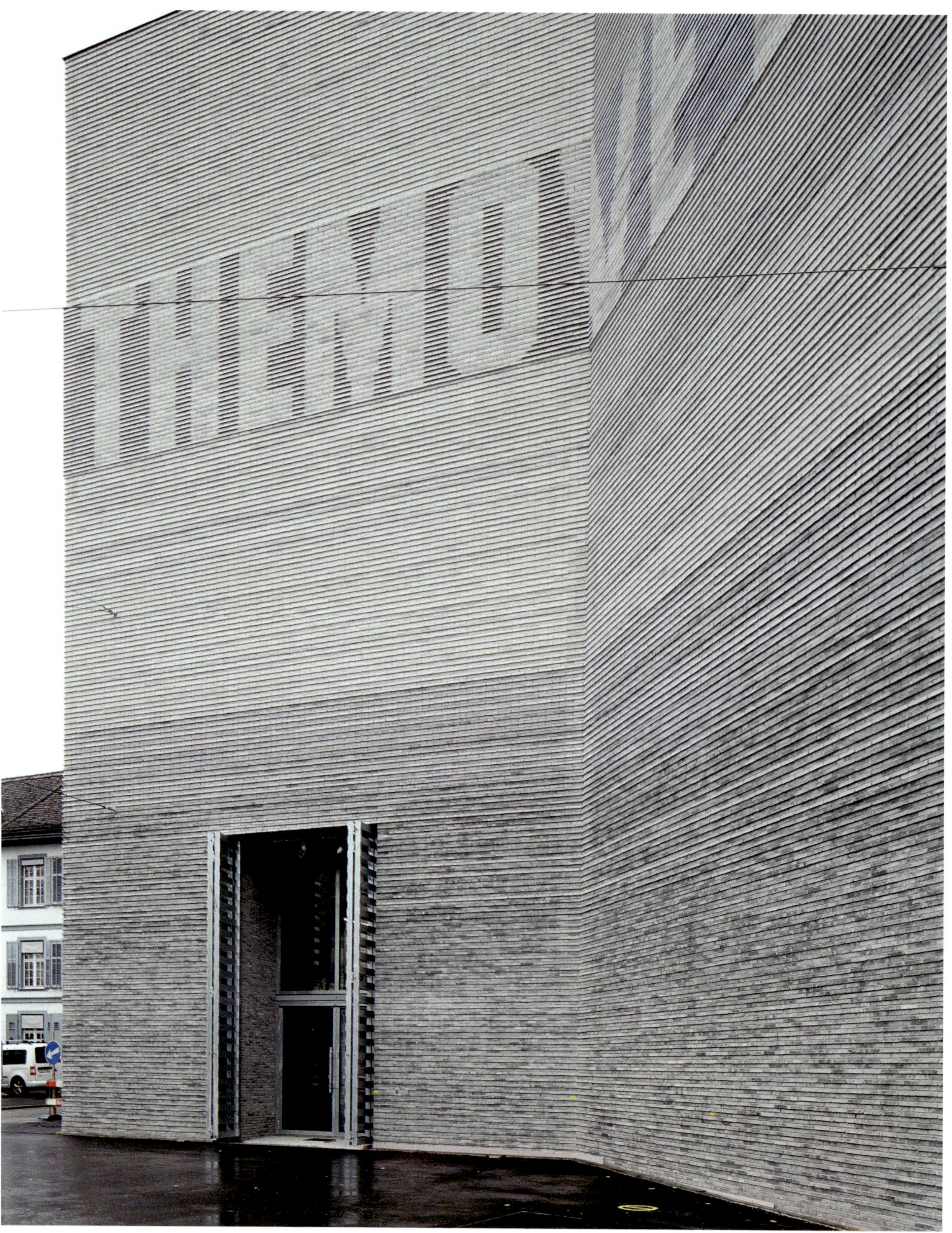

Facade with water-struck bricks, animated frieze with LEDs, entrance with galvanized steel doors

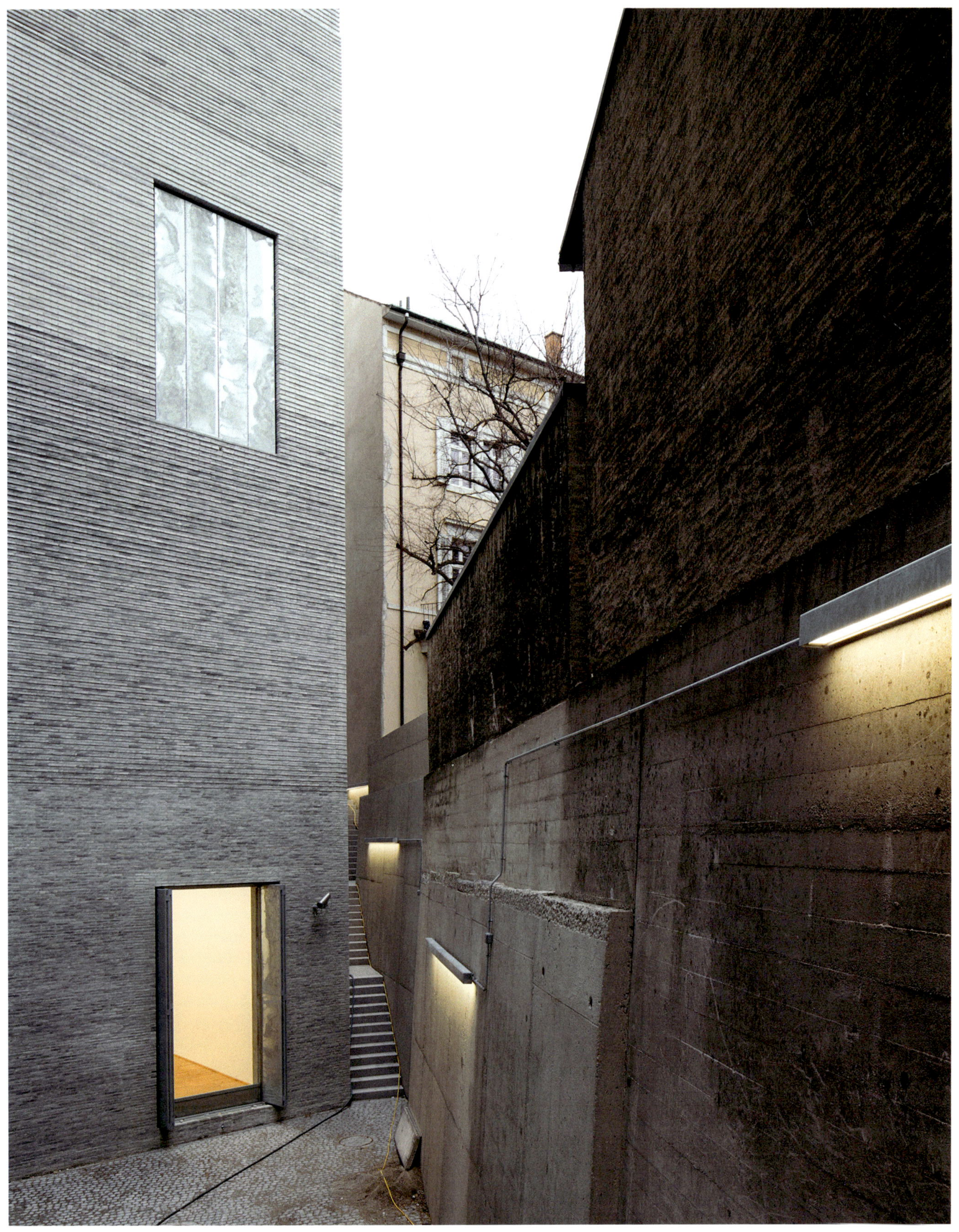

Small paved courtyard with glimpse into lower-level exhibition space U.3

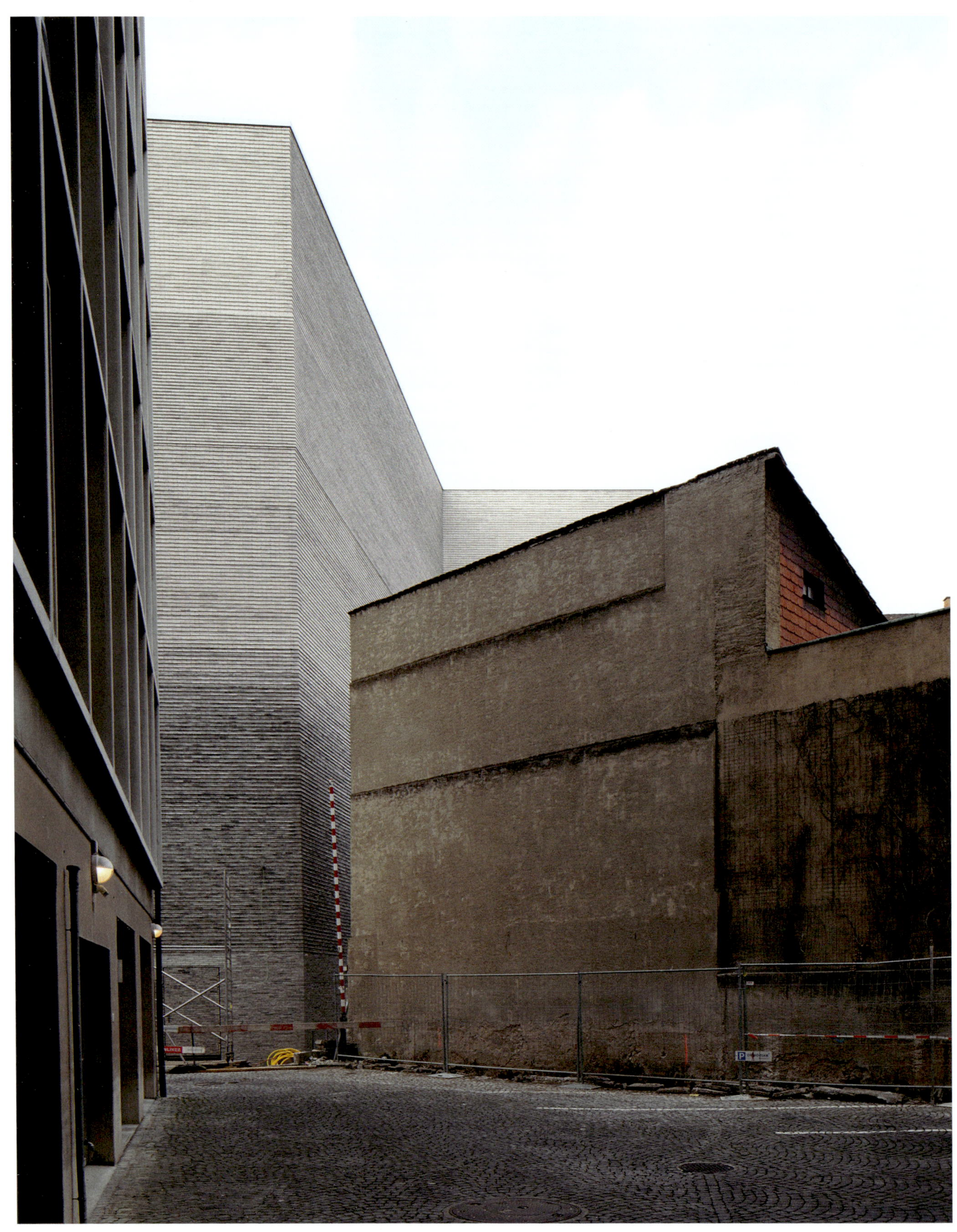

View onto the back of the new building with the neighboring Vorstadttheater

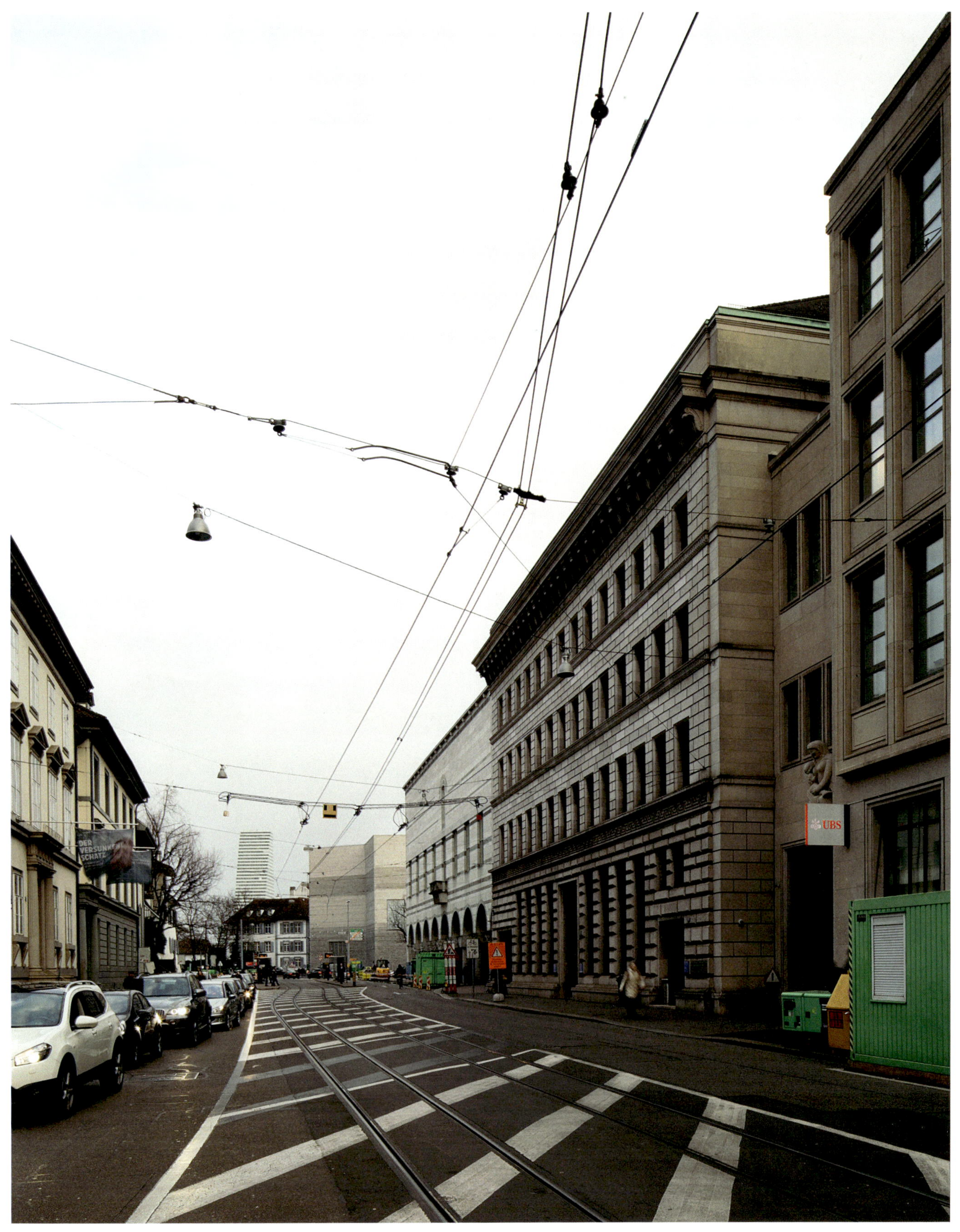

View from St. Alban-Graben of the Laurenzbau, main building, and new building

Kunstmuseum Basel, New Building

Edited by
Kunstmuseum Basel, Bernhard Mendes Bürgi

Editing
Salome Schnetz, Maren Stotz

Copyediting
Clare Manchester

Translations
Bronwen Saunders

Graphic design and typesetting
Studio Marie Lusa

Typeface
New Clarendon

Photography
Stefano Graziani

Color separation
REPROMAYER, Gesellschaft für die digitale Druck- und Medienvorstufe mbH, Reutlingen

Production
Christine Stäcker, Hatje Cantz

Paper
LuxoArtGloss, 150 g/m²

Printed by
Offsetdruckerei Karl Grammlich GmbH, Pliezhausen

Binding
Lachenmaier GmbH, Reutlingen

Published by
Hatje Cantz Verlag
Zeppelinstrasse 32
73760 Ostfildern
Germany
Tel. +49 711 4405-200
Fax +49 711 4405-220
www.hatjecantz.com
A Ganske Publishing Group company

Hatje Cantz books are available internationally at selected bookstores. For more information about our distribution partners please visit our homepage at www.hatjecantz.com

ISBN 978-3-7757-4091-3 (English)
ISBN 978-3-7757-4090-6 (German)

Printed in Germany

Cover illustration
Carl Andre, *Cedar Piece*, 1959/1964